SCRAMBLE!

a farce

David Wiltse

BROADWAY PLAY PUBLISHING INC
224 E 62nd St, NY, NY 10065
www.broadwayplaypub.com
info@broadwayplaypub.com

SCRAMBLE!

First printing: November 2010
I S B N: 978-0-88145-437-6

Book design: Marie Donovan
Typographic controls: Adobe InDesign
Typeface: Palatino
Printed and bound in the U S A

The world premiere of SCRAMBLE (as HATCHETMAN) was produced by Florida Stage (Lou Tyrrell, Producing Director; Nancy Barfnett, Managing Director) opening on 8 December 2006. The cast and creative contributors were:

JANE ....Susan Bennett
CARTER ....Todd Allen Durkin
JOHNSON...Shane Jacobsen
TEMPLE .... Beth McIntosh
OTIS... Colin McPhillamy
SAM .... Lisa Morgan

Director ....Louis Tyrrell
Scenic design... Mark Pirolo
Lighting design ....John McFadden
Costume design... Erin Amico

SCRAMBLE was produced at the Westport Country Playhouse (Artistic Director, Anne Keefe; Managing Director, Jodi Schoenbrun Carter) opening on 9 July 2008. The cast and creative contributors were:

JANE .... Rebecca Harris
CARTER ....Matthew Rauch
JOHNSON..Tom Beckett
TEMPLE .... Jennifer Mudge
OTIS... Colin McPhillamy
SAM ....Candy Buckley

Director ....Tracy Brigden
Set designer .... Jeff Cowie
Lighting designer ....Benjamin Stanton
Costume designer .... Ilona Somogyi

CHARACTERS

CARTER, *thirties, filled with frantic energy, usually in sexual overdrive*

TEMPLE, *thirties, very attractive, a cool but secretly insecure beauty*

JOHNSON, *twenties, thirties, bit of a nebbish, shy*

OTIS, *sixties and up, old family WASP but loopy, no memory*

JANE, *twenties, thirties, pathologically shy, seething with frustration*

SAM, *fifties, the lady boss, casually tyrannical, very sexual*

ACT ONE

Scene 1

(*The offices of a golf magazine. There are two playing areas,* CARTER's *office and* TEMPLE's *office.* TEMPLE's *office has two desks, two chairs.* CARTER's *office also has two desks and chairs. One of the desks,* CARTER's, *is somewhat bigger than the other. A wall, real or imagined, separates the two offices. Each office has one entryway exiting offstage, left or right, which we will call a regular door [although an open entry will make the comings and goings much easier] that leads eventually to the rest of the building, and a door upstage center that leads to the equipment room. The doors to the equipment room are painted a different color than everything else and are actual doors that open and close. The offstage equipment room connects the two offices to the rest of the building and each other but, as we will learn, its negotiation is difficult.*)

(*Time: The present*)

(*At rise:*)

(CARTER's *office.* CARTER, *thirties, is at work at his computer, typing away furiously—because he is furious and panicked. He works most of the time in a state of agitation just below rage, which is how he expresses his fear. Right now he's under pressure, harried, and irate.*)

(TEMPLE's *office:* TEMPLE, *thirties, beautiful, is at work at her desk.* JANE, *twenties or thirties, enters through regular door.* JANE *wears her hair up and big glasses on a chain around her neck like a stereotypical librarian. This is press day, the eleventh hour, and everyone is under great pressure.*)

TEMPLE: The print, where's the print?

JANE: (*Panicked*) Oh, my god! Oh my god! Oh my god! ...Which print?

TEMPLE: The one of the new golf ball with all the dimples.

JANE: Carter's got it!

TEMPLE: What's he doing, trying to mate with it?

JANE: Oh, my god...oh, my go—would he do that?

TEMPLE: Don't panic because we're going to press, Jane, I'm in charge.

JANE: You're not in charge. Who put you in charge?

TEMPLE: Go get the print from Carter and don't get all mumbley just because you're talking to a man—if we can call Carter that. I know you're soft on Carter but you've got to march in there and demand it from that over-sexed pea-brained mouth breather.

JANE: Oh, Temple, I couldn't do that...

TEMPLE: Oh, you poor thing, don't be frightened. Remember, there's nothing wrong with men that can't be cured by a set of pinking shears. Keep that in mind. Now fetch.

JANE: Why don't you do it?

TEMPLE: Jane, you know I have allergies. (*She taps her watch to show the fleeting time.*)

JANE: I don't have a problem with men! (*She exits, in a rush, fuming with frustration, through regular door.*)

(CARTER's *office*)

(CARTER *reviews his efforts on the computer screen and despairs.*)

CARTER: I can't do it! It's too hard, it's too much, it's too fast! You wouldn't treat a machine like this. (*He hates and pities himself for a moment, then resumes frantic typing as phone rings. Phone*) Yeh, Carter here! Yeh! Yeh! Yehyeh!... Six inches more!! Is that a joke?...I don't have six more inches in me, I'd need a transplant...No, you don't need another man for the job, I'll whip that right off for you... Five minutes to press time? No problem, Chief! (*Hangs up phone*) Nazi swine! While you're at it, why not take six inches of my large intestine? (*He resumes work, banging away frantically.*)

(*Enter* JANE, *racing in through regular door. She stops abruptly. She is always very shy in* CARTER'*s presence.*)

(*N B: When* JANE *speaks in the presence of men other than* OTIS, *she does it so fast that she is all but unintelligible. It is also mumbled. A suggestion of what she might be saying is printed as her dialogue, but it need not be understood by the audience.*)

JANE: (*Shyly*) Where'stheprint?

CARTER: What? What, Jane? What?

(JANE *tears through papers on his desk.*)

JANE: (*Restrained panic*) Ican'tfindit! I'mgettingpinkingshears!

(CARTER *strains to hear.*)

CARTER: Pinking shears? What does that mean?

JANE: (*Clearly*) Where's the print, you oversexed pea-brained mouth breather!

(CARTER *reacts with alarm, shuffles through papers on his desk, finds the photographic print, gives it to* JANE.)

(JOHNSON *enters* CARTER's *office through regular door and watches, quietly, intimidated by all the steam.* JOHNSON *is meek, unassuming, retiring by nature.*)

CARTER: (*Dignity hurt*) I am not a mouth breather.

JANE: (*Sincerely, mumbling*) Terriblysorrydidn'tmeantos aythat.

(*Enter* JOHNSON.)

(JANE *crosses towards door, nearly colliding with* JOHNSON.)

JOHNSON: Pardon me, I wonder...

(JANE *dips her head shyly, mutters.*)

JANE: Notimenotime. (*She points to watch indicating no time for chat. She exits.*)

CARTER: I can't do this! Woodward and Bernstein couldn't do this!

JOHNSON: (*Meekly*) Hello.

(CARTER *notices* JOHNSON *for the first time. He stares at him as if he can't quite comprehend his presence—which, in his present state, he can not.* CARTER *returns to his work, moaning and keening.* JOHNSON *stands uncertainly in the middle of the room, looking around. He gravitates towards golf trophies on a shelf.*)

JOHNSON: I was told to come in here and uh, sort of... wait?

(CARTER *wails and keens over his work.*)

CARTER: I can't do it! (*More furious typing*)

(TEMPLE's *office*)

(*Enter* JANE. *She drops the photo print on* TEMPLE's *desk.*)

TEMPLE: (*Condescending*) Oh, good job, Jane, good girl! You see what happens when you show them a confident front? If you want to be a successful executive like me you have to give the illusion that you know what you're doing.

JANE: You're not an executive. You're a staff writer, just like me.

TEMPLE: Well, not just like you.

(JANE *turns her back to* TEMPLE, *mouths the word "bitch!" then sits and resumes furious work.*)

(*Enter* OTIS. *He is dressed, always, as if he has just stopped by on his way to or from the golf course. This is simply his sartorial statement. He is sixty-ish, always pleasant but seemingly not always fully there. His speech has been influenced somewhat by the British without actually giving him an accent.*)

OTIS: Ah, the ladies.

(TEMPLE *gives him a chilly stare.*)

TEMPLE: Otis, press day.

OTIS: Quite.

(*Exit* OTIS, *chastened.* TEMPLE *resumes work.*)

(CARTER'*s office*)

CARTER: (*Of his work*) Puking Communist Fascist pig! Six inches! I deserve a Pulitzer for panic-induced writing...as if there were any other kind... (*Truly surprised*) I can't believe I did it... (*To* JOHNSON) If Jeffrey Dahmer calls, say I'm in the bathroom.

JOHNSON: Who...who's Jeffrey Dahmer?

(*Enter* OTIS. CARTER *does not acknowledge him.*)

CARTER: (*To* JOHNSON) New here, are you? The editor! Bloody in tooth and claw! (*He exits, angrily.*)

OTIS: Well, now.

JOHNSON: Yes.

(OTIS *waves his fingers as if he touched something hot.*)

OTIS: Whew!

JOHNSON: Yes, I guess so.

(OTIS *holds his right hand beside his ear, cocked and ready, as it were, to extend in greeting. A brief pause,* JOHNSON *doesn't know quite what's going on as* OTIS *struggles to remember his name.*)

OTIS: We've met, little trouble with your name. Don't help me. Tip of my tongue... Memory just a tad elusive. Italian name, was it? Al Fonso? Al Fresco?

JOHNSON: Me?

OTIS: Give us a clue. Al Gonquin, Al Dente, Al Layoop?

JOHNSON: I'm a little lost here.

OTIS: I know the feeling. Not to worry, it will come to you. Name tags in the clothing, does wonders...so, like working here, do you?

JOHNSON: It's been exciting so far.

OTIS: Exciting, oh, I'll say. Your friend Carter is quite a handful on press day. Lovely fella most of the time, don't get me wrong. He has that tongue, of course. Want to stay away from that. It shoots out there like a.... (*He folds his arm so his hand touches shoulder, then straightens it out quickly like a preying mantis' tongue. He does it again with an accompanying "phhtt" sound. Continuing*) Phhtt. Phhtt. What am I thinking of here?

JOHNSON: Aerobics?

OTIS: No, no, you miss the point. The animal with the enormously long tongue—not that Carter has a particularly long tongue—as far as I know—it's by way of a metaphor.

JOHNSON: Giraffe?

OTIS: No,no,no, that's neck. A giraffe is all neck. See here. (*He demonstrates again.*) Phhtt, phhtt. We're getting nowhere here. I don't need to tell you about your friend's tongue. You'd know better than I.

JOHNSON: He's not my friend, actually. I don't know anyone here. I ran into you in the lobby five minutes ago and you told me to wait in here.

OTIS: Thought I knew you. Birnberger! (*He goes through the cocking motion and offers his hand.*)

JOHNSON: No, my name is Johnson.

OTIS: I said it would come to you. Otis Birnberger here.

JOHNSON: Oh. Sorry. I'm Ben Johnson.

OTIS: Do you prefer Ken or Kenneth?

JOHNSON: Uh...Ben?

(*Enter* CARTER, *storming in, straight to computer. He reacts to the screen.*)

CARTER: (*Panicked*) Not clear! Not clear! (*To* JOHNSON) You! Don't stand there shaking like a dildo. Do you read? Take a look at this!

JOHNSON: Hi.

CARTER: What's unclear about it?

(TEMPLE's *office*)

TEMPLE: I'll be back. Try to remain calm.

JANE: (*Panicking*) I'm calm! Why wouldn't I be calm!

(*Exit* TEMPLE.)

(CARTER's *office*)

(JOHNSON *reads the screen, taps a few keys.* CARTER *looks at screen, back at* JOHNSON, *back at screen.*)

CARTER: Christ, a man off the streets can do it better than I can! I quit, I'm through, I'm going to get some post-its. (*He exits.*)

(JOHNSON *hesitates a moment, looking at screen, then quickly sits and types furiously for a moment as dialogue continues.*)

OTIS: Best to stay out of their way on press day.

(*Enter* TEMPLE)

TEMPLE: Ten minutes, Carter. Carter? ...Where is that lizard?

OTIS: Lizard! That's the word! Phtt! Phtt! (*He triumphantly demonstrates the folded arm-tongue motion to* JOHNSON.)

TEMPLE: Otis.

OTIS: Johnson here thought I meant a giraffe, if you can imagine.

TEMPLE: (*Sternly*) Otis!

OTIS: (*Instantly sobered*) Yes, Temple.

TEMPLE: Has Carter been running in and out every five minutes? If he makes us late again I'll see to it he's catheterized.

(*Both* JOHNSON *and* OTIS *wince at this notion.*)

OTIS: Temple, I'd like you to meet the new man....

(*Exit* TEMPLE.)

OTIS: Lovely thing, isn't she?

JOHNSON: Very pretty.

(JOHNSON *looks at* CARTER's *computer again. He can't help himself. He sits and types furiously for another few seconds before joining* OTIS. *The typing does not seem to require his attention and he faces* OTIS *as he types.*)

OTIS: An absolute ball-buster, of course.

JOHNSON: Oh, really? She seems uh...

OTIS: She wears Carter's like earrings. Carter follows her around bleating like a moon calf. Of course she

walks slowly enough so he doesn't get lost. The two
of them are just like Beatrice and...oh, the eggy dish...
Come along...Benedict. Madly in love with each other
and too stupid to know it.... Then again Jane's ga-ga as
a goat for Carter and he doesn't notice that. Sam would
pull a ligament to get at him, but you know Sam.

JOHNSON: N...no.

OTIS: Don't know how Carter will take to sharing the
office harem with a ladies' man like you, fast hands,
trysts in the copy room, eh, eh?
     You dog. Beware Carter's wrath, he's as jealous as...
the one with the horns?

JOHNSON: Goat? Devil? Cuckold?

OTIS: Not a zoologist, are you? Horns, horns.

JOHNSON: Elk? Moose? ...Unicorn?

OTIS: Santa Claus.

JOHNSON: Uh...elves? Sleigh? Beard?

OTIS: No, no, pay attention. The rabbit with the big
foot, a forest fire, mother lost, crying my eyes out, I can
see it clear as day, there stands the big fella atop a rock,
big eyes, cute tail—what do you call that?

JOHNSON: I, uh...

OTIS: Oh, what's that fella's name? Moustache, they
froze his body, all those amusement parks...

JOHNSON: Disney?

OTIS: Bambi!

JOHNSON: Deer?

OTIS: Stag! Not so hard, was it? You should do more
nature reading. Well, enough said, word to the wise.
Do you play golf at all?

JOHNSON: Not at all.

OTIS: Have a slice myself. Plague of a lifetime. Slice, do you?

JOHNSON: Well, no.

OTIS: Really? Envy you. We must play sometime. Just let me show you how things work. Equipment's in here, shoes, clubs, what have you, all you need and more. The closet's something of an innovative masterpiece. Designed it myself. Hub of the wheel. Not just a walk- in, a walk-through. Designed it for easy access from anywhere. Get to it from any office, use it as a shortcut. (*He struggles with the equipment door.*) Sticks occasionally. (*His frustration grows as he is unable to open the door to the closet. Finally he puts his shoulder to it, pushing as hard as he can.*) All together now.

(JOHNSON *joins him in pushing with his shoulder against the door. They finally give up.*)

OTIS: Yet sometimes as easy as one, two...whatever. Baffling.

(JOHNSON *pulls the door towards them rather than pushing. It opens immediately.*)

OTIS: Work out a lot, do you? Well, step in, step in.

(*Exit* JOHNSON *into equipment room.*)

JOHNSON: (*From inside*) Wow!

OTIS: Oh, yes. Equipment in here going back to Vardon's spoon. Light switch is just to your right—or possibly left. (*He fiddles with the handle trying to figure out what's wrong with it, then exits into the equipment room himself and closes the door behind them.*)

(*We hear the sound of equipment crashing in the equipment room.*)

(*Enter* CARTER. *He sits at the computer. He stares at the screen in astonishment.*)

CARTER: Elves? (*He tentatively pushes the send button.*)

(*Enter* TEMPLE.)

TEMPLE: Hurry up, you eunuch. Everyone else is done. If you make us late again I'll...

CARTER: Me? Me? I'm finished. We'd get things done a lot quicker if you didn't walk around distracting people with your beautiful...

TEMPLE: Say it, if you can afford the law suit.

(*Exit* TEMPLE.)

(*Exit* CARTER, *in pursuit.*)

(TEMPLE's *office*)

(*Exit* JANE, *through regular door.*)

(*The closet door rattles and shakes, there is the sound of more equipment falling and the door finally opens.*)

(*Enter* OTIS, *through equipment door, tumbling in amid a mild cascade of golf clubs.*)

(OTIS *has managed to get himself entangled in a two strap golf bag in such a way that it takes him the rest of the scene to free himself.*)

OTIS: Here we are, simple as that. Have to replace that light bulb. Otherwise...Johnson? Johnson?

(*Enter* TEMPLE, *enter* CARTER *in pursuit.*)

(OTIS *continues to struggle to disengage himself from the bag.*)

OTIS: Ah, children.

TEMPLE: (*To* CARTER) It was my idea to do that story on the greatest advance in golfing technology in forty years!

OTIS: (*Seeking assistance*) Little help here?

CARTER: The same greatest advance we wrote about six months ago.

(*A bell rings loudly.*)

CARTER: We've gone to press!

TEMPLE: We made it, Carter! We've gone to press!

(*A complete transformation. The stress and hostility vanish and* CARTER *and* TEMPLE *embrace joyously.*)

OTIS: Little help?

(CARTER *takes the collegial embrace a bit far and tries to hang on to* TEMPLE.)

CARTER: Care for a nooner?

TEMPLE: (*Throw away*) I'd sooner have an episiotomy.

CARTER: Perhaps another time.

OTIS: Anyone seen Johnson? Nondescript young chap, bit of an animal lover.

TEMPLE: I'm for a drink.

(OTIS, *entangled in the bag, gets in front of* TEMPLE.)

OTIS: Temple, a little help?

(TEMPLE *gives* OTIS *a fast embrace, paying no attention to his plight.* OTIS *struggles to get an arm around her to return the embrace.*)

TEMPLE: Another issue done on time, Otis!

OTIS: Never doubted you.

TEMPLE: You're sweet. (*She gives him a kiss on the cheek. She exits.*)

OTIS: (*Winks at* CARTER) Still have the robust musky charm.

CARTER: Get in my way with her and I'll crush you like a peeled grape.

OTIS: (*Upbeat*) Still, all's fair. I may have a look-in there.

(*Exit* CARTER.)

OTIS: Seen the new man, have you, Carter? ...Hope he's not afraid of the dark. Johnson? Johnson! (*Still hobbled by the golf bag, he exits back into equipment door. Again, a crash of clubs falling.)*

*(*CARTER's *office)*

(The equipment door opens and JOHNSON *hops in. One leg is stiff as a poker.)*

JOHNSON: Where am I? Mister Birnberger? (*He takes a step, limps, then turns like a dog after his tail, seeking something behind him. We can see that a golf club is inside the back of his pants running down one leg but it takes him some time to find and extract it. When free of the club, he sits at* CARTER's *computer and starts looking through it with great and growing interest. He takes a red notebook from under his shirt. It is attached to a chain around his neck. He takes notes in the notebook.)*

(Enter JANE, *rushing up to* JOHNSON *who hovers over the computer.* JANE, *mistaking him for* CARTER, *embraces him from behind.)*

JANE: Gone to press, gone to press!

*(*JOHNSON *scrambles guiltily to hide the red notebook in his shirt.)*

JOHNSON: I wasn't spying, honest!

*(*JANE *realizes it's not* CARTER.*)*

JANE: Oh. (*Mutters shyly*) Ithoughtyouwere...Carter.

JOHNSON: I know how it must look, but I was just... What did you say?

JANE: (*Mutters*) Idon'trememberIhavenoclue.

(A rattling of the equipment door, then enter OTIS *through equipment door, still trapped by the golf bag.)*

OTIS: Here we are then. Ah, Jane, you've met the new man.... Say hello, don't be shy.

JOHNSON: Hello. I'm Ben Johnson.

(JANE *mutters, extends a limp hand to* JOHNSON *while looking at* OTIS.)

JANE: I'mverypleasedtomeetyou.

JOHNSON: I'm sorry, I didn't catch...

(JANE *looks to* OTIS *for help, mumbles again.*)

JANE: I'mJaneCarew.

OTIS: (*Translating*) How do you do, I'm Jane Carew. Welcome aboard. We'll do everything we can to make your stay a pleasant one.

(JOHNSON *is bewildered, doesn't know whom to address.*)

JOHNSON: Uh, thank you, my name is Ben Johnson and I look forward to working with you.

JANE: Metoo.

OTIS: (*Translating*) One big happy family here, you'll fit right in.

JOHNSON: I'm so glad to hear that. I've always wanted a family...

(OTIS *now translates for* JOHNSON *as well.*)

OTIS: (*To* JANE) Says he's pleased as punch. Lacks the odd social skill but his heart is pure.

JOHNSON: Uh, uh, uh... (*He gestures that* OTIS *has it somewhat wrong.*)

JANE: That'stoobadI'msorrytohearit.

OTIS: (*Translating*) Don't expect sympathy from me, you whey-faced toad, I have my own problems.

JANE: Ididn'tsaythat!

OTIS: (*Laughs*) Sorry, got that wrong.

(JANE *crosses towards exit.*)

JOHNSON: Wait!

(*Exit* JANE.)

(JOHNSON *is not sure what's just happened.*)

OTIS: Lovely girl, Jane. Pathologically shy around men at first, but you two certainly seem to be hitting it off.

JOHNSON: I wasn't quite sure what...

OTIS: Fast mover, eh, Johnson? Must be a married man.

JOHNSON: No, I...

OTIS: Ah, legion of pals and chums, that sort of thing. That's the modern way.... Little help here?

(JOHNSON *helps* OTIS *extricate himself.*)

JOHNSON: Actually, I don't have any friends, actually. People don't warm to me immediately, I don't know why.

OTIS: Personality. Bit of a cold fish, simple clod, something on that order.

JOHNSON: But underneath, I'm really...

OTIS: Warm, loving, devoted, loyal. The old story, kiss a toad, get a prince—but—fear of warts.

(JOHNSON *instinctively, and briefly, covers his crotch at the mention of warts.*)

OTIS: You'll fit right in here, Johnson.

JOHNSON: Really? Oh, I hope so. I really want to make some friends.

OTIS: One big happy family in this office. Everyone as friendly as lemmings in a hole.

JOHNSON: I just hope they'll let me join them. I feel like an orphan most of the time.

OTIS: An orphan? Good heavens. Not even a mother?

JOHNSON: Not that I recall.

OTIS: You should pay attention to these things. Older woman, larger than yourself, smells of talcum powder and sour milk.

JOHNSON: I was raised in foster homes. That's why I tend to just blend into the wallpaper. I get very intimidated in certain situations, get a little tongue-tied, can't quite express myself.

OTIS: Seem to be nattering on interminably to me.

JOHNSON: I feel strangely comfortable with you.

OTIS: Because I'm recently orphaned myself, you know. Lost the Mater only last month. Knew her my whole life. Bereft.

JOHNSON: I'm very sorry.

OTIS: Thank you, Ken. Just a pair of waifs, eh? Buffeted by fate. We must stick together in this cruel world... Plunge into work, that's the thing. This office is the perfect place for the lost and lonely. Look at Jane. Lone as a widowed goose to the naked eye, but underneath that hapless exterior...

JOHNSON: She's a widow?

OTIS: Jane? Good Lord, is she? Terrible thing, one so young, forced to dress in black the rest of her days, squat in the corner making tortillas... Oh, you and Jane will hit it off like cheese and crackers. Being a widow, bound to lower her standards.

JOHNSON: No, I don't uh...

OTIS: Oh, too good for her, are you, Mister Hoity-toity?... (*Of golf bag*) What's this doing here?

JOHNSON: (*To change the subject*) What is your job here exactly, Mister Birnberger?

OTIS: I'll just return this to the proper place then tell you all about it. (*He takes the golf bag to equipment door, makes a great effort to open it and, by chance, pulls it the proper way. He nearly falls, recovers and exits through the equipment door, pulling it closed behind him.*)

(*We hear the sound of crashing equipment.*)

(*Enter* CARTER *hurriedly. He stops abruptly, surprised to see* JOHNSON.)

CARTER: Christ! I thought you were part of the woodwork.

JOHNSON: I know. I'm Ben Johnson. We met earlier. You called me dildo.

CARTER: (*Examines him*) I can see that, but I don't remember you.

JOHNSON: People frequently don't...

(*Enter* TEMPLE.)

CARTER: Ah, it's daybreak and Juliet is the sun.

TEMPLE: Take a pill or something, Carter. Who are you?

JOHNSON: I'm Ben J...

CARTER: He must be the replacement for Gupta Singh.

TEMPLE: I miss Gupta. He was the only one here who played golf...poor Gupta.

JOHNSON: What...what happened to him?

TEMPLE: He was last seen with Sam...and never again.

CARTER: All we ever found was his left shoe and the inseam of his pants.

JOHNSON: Sam?

CARTER: More like Son of Sam, if you follow.

JOHNSON: (*Terrified*) Son of Sam?

(CARTER *spits ritually through his fingers.*)

CARTER: Never speak the name of the devil aloud, man!

TEMPLE: Sam's after Carter, so you'll be safe. Keep your eye on the gates to the city. Carter's head will be there on a pike in no time.

JOHNSON: But who, who...

TEMPLE: (*To* CARTER) Did I see Otis earlier wrestling with a golf bag?

CARTER: Now that you mention it...didn't seem remarkable at the time.

JOHNSON: Ah, Mister Birnberger. He seems very... What is his job, exactly?

CARTER: Job? Would you trust Otis with a job? Otis is the son of the founder of the magazine, Iron Jack Birnberger of blessed memory.

TEMPLE: Iron Jack is our hero. He fought back a takeover attempt by a big publishing corporation and sold forty percent of his ownership just to keep the magazine private.

CARTER: He kept our little family intact, so we tolerate Otis out of respect to his memory.

TEMPLE: He just hangs around. Sort of like Carter, but he doesn't get in the way as much.

CARTER: You always hurt the one you love.

TEMPLE: (*To* JOHNSON) Listen, Todd, if you're going to be working here you should know that I'm always on the look-out for fresh ideas, really innovative approaches to golf instruction, that sort of thing. Come straight to me with any thoughts, we'll work them up together.

CARTER: Better yet, come to me and I'll go to Temple. We have this rapport.

TEMPLE: You wish.

JOHNSON: But surely we're all members of the same editorial family. It would be like sharing with your brothers and sisters.

TEMPLE: Ah, but there's always that one sister who steals your clothes and sleeps with your boy friend.

JOHNSON: Really?

TEMPLE: Trust no one.

JOHNSON: Oh, never say that. All my life I have yearned for the comfort and security of a family. I need people who care about me, listen to me, want to be with me, and yet, somehow, in my life and work I am never even noticed. I, I, I, I, I...

CARTER: Just skip that part.

TEMPLE: Sing. People don't stutter when they sing.

JOHNSON: I...I...I...

TEMPLE: (*Command voice*) Sing!

JOHNSON: (*Singing*) Haarooo! The continental, it's very daring/the continental, it's strictly *entre nous.*

(CARTER *and* TEMPLE *look on, baffled.*)

CARTER: At least he isn't stuttering.

(*Enter* JANE *in a near panic.*)

JANE: Runforyourlivesshe'sontheway!... (*Clearly*) Sam!

(*General panic*)

TEMPLE: Everyone stay calm.

JANE: (*To* TEMPLE) Hide me.

CARTER: You!? Hide me!

JOHNSON: What, what?

TEMPLE: (*To* JOHNSON) For god's sake, don't pee down your leg the way Carter does.

CARTER: I had an infection! I'm going to get some paper clips! (*He hurries towards the door, but he is too late.*)

(*Enter* SAM. CARTER *recoils into the room.* SAM *is a woman in her fifties. She does not appear to be so frightening.*)

SAM: Ah, here you all are, huddled together for comfort. (*She eyes the group, seeing but not seeing*

JOHNSON.) There seem to be more of you than usual but with all the cowering it's hard to tell.

(JANE *and* CARTER *point trembling fingers towards* JOHNSON. JOHNSON *raises a trembling hand.* SAM *regards him with a speculative eye. It should be noted that* SAM *is sexually voracious.*)

SAM: (*Seductively*) What's this scratching at my door?

JOHNSON: N...new man.

SAM: Yes, that's right, you're here to fill in for dear departed Gupta, aren't you? There's nothing like a new man to change your outlook. Isn't that right, Jane?

JANE: (*Meaning me?!*) Murfff?!

SAM: We must get acquainted, you can tell me your interests. Do you ride?

JOHNSON: Ma...Ma...Ma'am?

SAM: Horses are so like people, don't you find? Take young Carter there, skittish as a colt, afraid of the saddle, doesn't know what's good for him...but a show pony like yourself, you'll run rings around him in no time, won't you, new man?

JOHNSON: (*Sings*) Harooo, the continental...

SAM: We'll discuss that later...Do you know anything about golf?

JOHNSON: N...n...nothing.

SAM: Good, you won't be bothered by preconceptions. Maybe we'll get some real writing done around here, eh Carter? Oh, and Carter, one small thing?

CARTER: Ja wohl?

SAM: The feature article? How shall I put this. Your first draft, was that a literal translation from some language—which you do not speak? Urdu, perhaps?

CARTER: You felt it lacked felicity of phrasing?

SAM: (*Sexual innuendo*) Then when I got—stern—with you, you suddenly got up for it. Your final rewrite was a veritable explosion. Could it be you need more discipline?

CARTER: (*Trying to laugh*) Just the occasional lash, ha-ha.

SAM: Is that what you need to spur you on? I can do that...I'm always happy to help you when you can't rise to the occasion, Carter.

CARTER: So grateful.

SAM: The rest of you barely scraped by, as usual. But it's your last free ride, there are going to be changes around here. The magazine's been put on the market, there's a corporation sniffing around, I'm told. Brush will be cleared, deadwood stacked and burned. Only the strong will survive. And if I have to throw the more egregiously incompetent among you under the bus to maintain my control of this vehicle, consider yourself part of the pavement.

(*Enter* OTIS *from the equipment door, stumbling in, accompanied by a crash of clubs behind him.*)

OTIS: Simple as that.

SAM: Anything you care to add, Otis?

OTIS: (*Lost*) Ahhh.... Re...?

SAM: Remember, new man, any questions, any problems, my door is always open...wide open. Any time. Isn't that right, Carter?

JOHNSON: Thank you, Ma'am.

SAM: Just call me Sam, we're all family here.

JOHNSON: I'm so glad to hear that. A family is all....all... all.. (*Sings*) All I need is love, love/love is all I need.

(*Exit* SAM.)

JOHNSON: She seems very nice.

TEMPLE: (*Terror*) We're going to be sold to a corporation? They'll bring in new executives!

CARTER: They'll want real writers!

JANE: Ican'tworkanywhereelse!

TEMPLE: They'll want new ideas!

CARTER: They'll fire the staff! We're doomed!

TEMPLE: I can't afford to lose this job, I have allergies!

CARTER: I'll provide for you. Throw yourself on my charity.

TEMPLE: That's what you call it.

JANE: (*Doleful*) Who'lltakecareofmymother?

TEMPLE: ...Oh, Jane, you thing. Who will ever hire you?

JANE: (*Indignant*) Murf?! Whataboutyou?

CARTER: We have to stay united. We're all in this together. We're a team.

JOHNSON: (*Brightly*) Like siblings!

(*The others all look at* JOHNSON *for a moment, then turn back to each other.*)

CARTER: We will provide each other with moral support. (*To* TEMPLE) I will comfort you... (*He puts a consoling arm around* TEMPLE.) And Jane you can...

(JANE *leans into* CARTER.)

CARTER: (*Continuing*) ...We'll work something out. Let's go get some Mexican and make a plan.

TEMPLE: I'm sure I'll have some ideas by then.

CARTER: Nothing like a Margarita, a cold beer and a big plate of previously eaten beans to make you think.

(*They start towards the exit,* CARTER *with his arm around* TEMPLE, JANE *wrapped around* CARTER's *waist.*)

OTIS: Oh, I say, I quite fancy...

(TEMPLE *pushes* CARTER's *arm away.* JANE *leans into him until* CARTER *becomes aware of her and removes her arms from him.*)

(*Exit* TEMPLE, CARTER, JANE.)

OTIS: (*Deflated*) ...a drink myself. (*To* JOHNSON) A bit clannish at times, nothing personal...Make the best of a bad bargain though. You and I together, thick and thin. Two Musketeers, one for all, and, uh, the other thing. Care for Mexican?

JOHNSON: My stomach's a little delicate. I have quite a reaction to Mexican food.

OTIS: Runny mucus, diarrhea?

JOHNSON: Projectile vomiting.

OTIS: Should make for a change. Shall we?

(*Enter* JANE. *She eyeballs them both.* OTIS *preens hopefully. She points to* OTIS.)

JANE: Ican'ttalkinfrontofCarter.

OTIS: (*To* JOHNSON) In some need of a translator. (*To* JANE) Right you are, my dear. Didn't wish to impose myself. All part of the family though, aren't we?

(*Exit* OTIS *and* JANE.)

(JOHNSON *is left. Alone again. Feeling very sorry for himself, he sighs voluminously, then sags into dejection. After a moment he takes the red notebook from his shirt and begins to scribble intensely.*)

(*Blackout*)

Scene 2

(*Time: A few days later*)

(*The offices are empty.*)

(TEMPLE's *office*)

(*Enter* CARTER. *He peers in, then enters the office on tip toe. He holds a bouquet of roses. He looks for something to put them in, finds nothing, empties some pencils from a mug on* TEMPLE's *desk and puts the flowers in it.*)

(CARTER *then takes a collection of inscribed Post-its from his pocket and pastes them on objects in Temple's work space. He hears a noise off of someone approaching.* CARTER *dashes into the equipment door.*)

(*Exit* CARTER *through equipment door.*)

(*Enter* TEMPLE. *She notices the roses.*)

TEMPLE: Flowers? Carter will never learn. (*She sneezes, then takes a deep breath, holds it, and puts the roses on* JANE's *desk then notices the Post-its. She collects and reads them as she goes.*)

TEMPLE: (*Continuing; reading*) Must...your...disdain... keep us...apart? ...Then shrivel, fade and die...my... heart. (*She negligently drops the accumulated Post-its on* JANE's *desk.*)

TEMPLE: (*Continuing*) Not without appeal, in an over-reaching glandular way.

(CARTER's *office*)

(*We hear off a sound of crashing equipment.*)

(*Enter* CARTER *through the equipment door. He kicks some equipment back into the equipment room, then crosses to his desk. He stretches, looks at the computer screen, lifts his hands as if to write, then falls instantly asleep.*)

(TEMPLE's *office*)

(SAM *enters.*)

SAM: Temple...

TEMPLE: Yes, Sam?

SAM: The old clock on the wall tells me it's time to do the article on golf fashion again. Care to take a whack at that?

TEMPLE: I think my talents could be better used than writing women's articles—say in an executive position as managing editor—which would allow me to oversee the others and relieve your own work burden.

SAM: Ah, you feel I'm giving you "women's work". You feel demeaned and insulted. You yearn for advancement beyond your skill level. I admire ambition, no matter how laughably overreaching. Of course such a post would require a good deal of creative thinking, coming up with new ideas for articles and series and so forth. Any new ideas, Temple?

TEMPLE: The article on golf tees was mine.

SAM: Memorable. Readership soared.

TEMPLE: Of course I have many other articles in various stages of development. I wouldn't want to give them to you prematurely.

SAM: There's no satisfaction when things are premature, it's true...but isn't it curious that the new man has been here only a couple days and yet he's spewing ideas like a garden hose. Even Jane has ideas—many of them weird and incoherent to be sure—but you seem to have none.

TEMPLE: I have tons of ideas! I'm just refining them.

SAM: I hope you have them ready by the time the hatchet man arrives.

TEMPLE: The hatchet man?

SAM: When ownership changes there's always a hatchet man. He slips in like a bad odor and decides who's pulling his weight and who's getting by on her youth and tartish good looks. Oh, and then the heads roll, there's blood running in the gunnels. We'd hate to lose someone with your youth and tartish good looks just because you haven't got an original thought in your head.... So I'll give the article on fashion to Jane, shall I? She likes a good insult, hardly notices.

TEMPLE: I'll do it.

SAM: She may write about "a dozen ways to dress in burlap", but it'll be interesting...

TEMPLE: I want to do it.

SAM: Jane will be disappointed, but it's yours.

(SAM *exits, leaving* TEMPLE *to fume.*)

TEMPLE: Pustulant cow.

(JANE *enters on* TEMPLE's *line and is briefly taken aback. She sees the roses on her desk.* JANE *picks up the roses and approaches* TEMPLE.)

JANE: What's this?

TEMPLE: (*With disgust*) From Carter.

JANE: (*Puzzled*) From Carter?

(*Thrilled,* JANE *does a little whirl, bringing the flowers close to* TEMPLE.)

TEMPLE: Keep those away from me, you know how allergic I am.... Now I have to take a pill. (*She exits.*)

(JANE *reads the Post-its that are now out of sequence.*)

JANE: (*Reading*) Your...heart...must...shrivel fade and die. (*Normal*) That is so sweet.... Oh, Carter, you care! (*She waltzes with the flowers, then puts them on her desk and addresses the imaginary* CARTER.) Take me you fool! (*With her back to the audience, she wraps her arms around*

her self so that it looks as if someone else were kissing her,
running his hand through her hair, etc.) No, you mustn't!
(As CARTER) I must have you! *(As* JANE) Very well...
Oh, you great, greedy beast!

(TEMPLE *enters.*)

TEMPLE: Who you talking to?

JANE: No one!

TEMPLE: You're losing it, Jane.

JANE: Oh, I was just, uh, thinking what to say to my
man.

TEMPLE: You have a man? Who is it?

JANE: Oh, no one.

TEMPLE: Well, imaginary friends are good, too. You
know, you wouldn't look blander than tofu if you let
down your hair and took off those glasses. *(She whips*
off JANE's *glasses.)* There!

(JANE *is blind as a bat without her glasses. She staggers*
around with her hands in front of her, groping for something
to hold on to.)

JANE: Temple? Temple?

TEMPLE: Never mind, bad idea. *(She returns the glasses*
to JANE.) Just remember, Jane, you have to set the terms
with a man right at the beginning. Let him know there
are boundaries. I find that if you start things off by
giving him this... *(She thrusts a fist upward, slapping the*
other hand to her bicep in the sign of "up yours".) ...it tells
him where he stands.

JANE: But I could never do that.

TEMPLE: Men will get in the way of your career if you
let them think you're available.

JANE: I don't have a career, I'm taking care of my
mother.

TEMPLE: Let her out of the attic, Jane. It's time.... If you want to get ahead, you have to project an image of strength and independence. (*She does it again, this time with bared teeth and a snarl.*)

JANE: It seems—hostile—somehow.

TEMPLE: Works for me. Remember, Jane, when the hatchet man comes you'll have to make some changes. Maybe even— speak.

JANE: Oh, I, I don't see how I could...

TEMPLE: Just a thought, Jane. No need to panic. (*She exits.*)

JANE: I'm not panicked!

(CARTER's *office*)

(*Enter* JOHNSON. *He is carrying coffee in a styrofoam cup and pastry on a napkin for* CARTER. *He puts them down next to sleeping* CARTER, *tip toes to his desk and removes the red notebook from his shirt. He scribbles in the notebook.*)

(CARTER *awakens,* JOHNSON *hurriedly and clumsily stuffs the red notebook back in his shirt.*)

CARTER: So, Johnson, ever have a woman in a sleeping bag...on the back of a motorcycle...during a pollen alert?

JOHNSON: Uh...I brought your coffee.

CARTER: Janice Markowitz, camp Muckabout, August, 1989. (*He takes the coffee and pastry.*) No plate?

JOHNSON: Do you usually nap at work?

CARTER: The beauty of working at a monthly magazine is that nothing gets done for the first three weeks before press time.... It's our company culture.

JOHNSON: Oh, I see.

SAM: (*Off; seductively*) Ohhh, Cart-er!

(CARTER *reacts with horror*.)

CARTER: (*To* JOHNSON) It's the Butcher of Buchenwald.
I'm going for printer paper!

SAM: (*Off*) Ohhh, Carter-Warter...

(CARTER *tries to hide but there is no place to conceal himself.*
He positions JOHNSON *in front of him.* JOHNSON *is now*
terrified, too.)

CARTER: Quick, pretend you're me.

(*Enter* SAM.)

SAM: Cart... Oh, new man. Seen Carter around?

JOHNSON: I...I...I...I... (*Sings*) Harooo, the continental...

SAM: You don't need to go into detail. ...Oh, Carter, is
that you I see cowering like the cutest little bunny on
the edge of his hidey hole?

CARTER: Oh, hi there, Chief. Didn't hear you come in.
Wrapped up in my work.

(SAM *sits on* CARTER's *desk, crosses her legs in what she*
considers a provocative manner. CARTER *grips* JOHNSON
and makes a sub-vocal apprehensive noise.)

SAM: Well, now, Carter.

CARTER: At your service.

SAM: Carter, Carter.

CARTER: We aim to please. No job too small.

(SAM *looks at the computer screen*.)

SAM: I wonder, Carter, if you might explain your
reputed humor piece about golfing in Afghanistan.

CARTER: How much do you like it?

SAM: What does it mean, why have you done it, what
possessed you to write it? Or, to put it another way,
change it completely, would you? Make it humorous.
Just as a favor, all right, Carter?

CARTER: Yes, sir, I'll get right on it!

SAM: Thank you. And new man, nice work on that travel piece. Travel writing is so often—flaccid—but yours touched me in all the right places. Keep it Up.

JOHNSON: Thank you.

(*Exit* SAM.)

CARTER: (*Fiercely mocking*) Thank you! Thank you! Christ, Johnson, why don't you lick her filthy boots while you're at it! Why not prostrate yourself in front of her? I, for one, will not kiss her...

(*Enter* SAM, *again*.)

SAM: And Carter...

CARTER: *Ja wohl, mein Herr!*

SAM: If I could have that rewrite before lunch.

CARTER: Your slightest wish, my liege.

SAM: You know, Carter, the hatchet man is on his way. He won't be nearly as patient and understanding as I am.... Of course I could put in a good word for you—if I could think what it was. If you have anything to say for yourself, you know where to find me.... My door is always open...and of course we can close it, if need be.... Meanwhile, fix the—uh—specimen—you left in the computer.

CARTER: *Mein Kommandant.*

(SAM *exits.* CARTER *peers out the door to make sure she's really gone.*)

CARTER: Change it! It's constructed like a Swiss watch. I couldn't redo this before next week!

JOHNSON: Would you like me to look at it? (*He looks at computer screen.*)

CARTER: She has me in her sights, my fate is sealed, I'm dead as cheese. If Sam doesn't get rid of me the

hatchet man will... I'll tell you the truth, I deserve it. I
can't write, I'm not a writer. I might as well squat on
the screen and get it over with. And the worst part is, I
love this magazine. My father used to read it. I'd watch
him poring over the instruction series and he'd nod his
head and get out of his chair and try Ben Hogan's test
tip, and he'd nod his head again. He found truth in the
glossy pages of our little book.

He couldn't find it in his life, but here, in the tired
advice of some hack like me writing the same shop-
worn stuff we write today he glimpsed an eternal
verity about the swing path and the flight of the ball.
I want to continue that tradition, Johnson, I want
this magazine to be a beacon for those troubled in
mind and restless in spirit to turn to! I want it to be
more than just a golf magazine, I want it to be Truth!
...Christ, that's banal! I'm a halfwit!

JOHNSON: That's such a beautiful sentiment, Carter!

CARTER: Well, it's all over, I've failed, when the hatchet
man comes he'll lop me off like a goiter. I'll die in a
ditch.

JOHNSON: Your ideas are good, it's the way you express
them.

CARTER: You mean the words. See, that's the part about
writing that always gets me. It's no use, I'm for the
crapper.

JOHNSON: May I?

CARTER: What harm could you do?

(JOHNSON *types with incredible speed.*)

CARTER: Who are you, Mozart?

(TEMPLE's *office*)

(JANE *is mooning about the flowers.*)

(*Enter* OTIS.)

OTIS: Ah, Jane. Interesting occurrence at the golf course...

JANE: Not now, Otis.

OTIS: Righty-oh. (*He exits.*)

(CARTER's *office*)

(*With a flourish* JOHNSON *finishes typing and presses the send key.*)

CARTER: You took out all the good stuff.

JOHNSON: Logic doesn't matter in comedy, speed is what counts. A man with his foot stuck in a bucket is better than ten pages of clever dialogue.

CARTER: It doesn't matter. Sam will never like anything with my name attached to it. I won't sleep with her, that's why she hates me.... Well, I may have to....

JOHNSON: You'd do that?

CARTER: To keep my job? I'm a writer, Johnson, I'm basically unemployable...I need her to put in a good word for me with the hatchet man—well, a whole damn thesaurus.

JOHNSON: Still...isn't sex in the workplace dangerous?

CARTER: Well, don't do it while operating heavy machinery.

   I'm all for it in theory but I want to be sure I'll survive it ungelded. Sam is a horsewoman, man! Remember Gupta! She'll ride me like a palomino. Think of the spurs, Johnson, good god the spurs!

JOHNSON: But...is sex in the office a good idea in general?

CARTER: Got a better one?

(OTIS *enters.*)

OTIS: Ah, lads...

CARTER: Otis, sex in the office, what say?

OTIS: Good lord, where? Horny as a hatrack myself. Even thinking about the girl in accounting, the grateful one. What's her name, some kind of antelope.... Oh, I can see them now, bounding, bounding.

CARTER: Giselle.

OTIS: The very same. I was thinking only today...

CARTER: Not now, Otis.

OTIS: Quite right, nose to the grindstone. Carry on. (*He exits.*)

CARTER: Need I say more? The idea appeals even to the halt, the lame and those packed in salt.

JOHNSON: But—with someone you work with, isn't that harassment?

CARTER: Good God, man, you don't harass them. You woo them. You're with these people eight hours a day, five days a week, you don't spend that much time with your family. Look at yourself, Johnson. You want to fit in, right?

JOHNSON: Oh, yes, very much.

CARTER: You want to be part of the group, one of the family, you want to be interesting, you want people talking about you behind your back. What would you say is your primary characteristic in most people's mind? Boring, tedious, clueless? Am I close?

JOHNSON: Well, I would hope...yeah, something like that.

CARTER: Have an affair, you'll be interesting immediately.

JOHNSON: Oh, I wouldn't know how to do that. I'm very shy around women.

CARTER: Couldn't be simpler. Show genuine interest in her life. Inquire about her health, her state of mind, her family and her pets, especially the pets she thinks are talking to her. Learn to say, "I know, I know" as if you knew. Figure out the color of her eyes and when you forget, ask somebody, never guess, the odds are bad. Let her know you truly care about her, no detail too small or incomprehensible. If all that fails, try alcohol... So, who do you like, Giselle?

JOHNSON: Well, I like...

CARTER: True, she braids her armpits, we feed her with a stick, but once she's sedated....

JOHNSON: Well, I thought...

CARTER: How about Jane? She's nice, don't you think?

JOHNSON: Very nice.

CARTER: Possibly mental, of course, but think of her as a woodland creature—probably lives in a moss- lined hole—timid, harmless, mute, and that gives you more time to talk about yourself.

JOHNSON: Oh, there's nothing much I can say about myself.

CARTER: I've noticed that. You hiding something? You in witness protection?

JOHNSON: My only life is here, in the office.

CARTER: Well, it's a start. I'm sure Giselle would be grateful to hear that much. She finds the human voice soothing.

JOHNSON: Temple seems to like me...

CARTER: What!?

JOHNSON: She's always asking if I have any ideas about...

CARTER: Temple is mine!

JOHNSON: But...she doesn't care for you.

CARTER: Of course she cares for me!

JOHNSON: She doesn't act like it.

CARTER: That's how they show it. Have you ever even talked to a woman?

JOHNSON: Temple and I talk quite a bit.

CARTER: (*Crumbling*) She talks to you? Why? What do you do? Tell me, tell me. I would give a bowel to have her like me back. Tell me what you do.

JOHNSON: Sort of...nothing.

CARTER: (*Himself again*) Nothing? You do nothing? I can't do that, you imbecile. I'm hyperactive!

JOHNSON: I guess it works because we get along real well...

CARTER: Let me be blunt. If you go anywhere near Temple, I will eat you. Belt and all.

JOHNSON: You asked me who I should have sex with...

CARTER: Out of my office! Out, out, I banish you.... Argh!

JOHNSON: What's wrong?

(CARTER's *leg is in great pain. He hops a bit, howling.*)

CARTER: (*in pain*) Old football injury...trick knee.

JOHNSON: What can I do?

CARTER: Why not drive a spike in it, you Judas.... Out, I want you out of here! Out! Out!

JOHNSON: Should I call someone?

CARTER: Call the hatchet man and tell him to get rid of you before I do, because it won't be pretty. Out, out, out, you traitorous little swine!

(CARTER *comes after* JOHNSON, *hands stretched out to strangle him, lurching as he walks—a bit like Frankenstein. Johnson runs off in fright.*)

(JOHNSON *exits.*)

(CARTER *limps about a bit, waggling his leg, trying to get the knee back in place then proceeds to scribble things on Post-its and stick them to* JOHNSON's *computer and other furniture, making a trail to* CARTER's *terminal screen where he triumphantly posts the last one. He reads them aloud as he writes and sticks.*)

CARTER: Quisling, this treachery...shall not pass... pucker up and kiss my...rosy red...

(TEMPLE *enters as* CARTER *writes and posts the last, unspoken, note.*)

TEMPLE: So, Carter, still practicing self-abuse?

CARTER: Some things you can't be too good at.

TEMPLE: Stay with it, you'll figure it out. (*She perches on his desk, crosses her legs, displays a great deal of seductive leg.*)

CARTER: (*Responding to her leg*) Oh, roast me over slow coals.

TEMPLE: Yes, I know. Where's Todd?

CARTER: He's gone to deal with his herpes. What do you want with that little newt that I can't give you? Name it and it's yours.

TEMPLE: New ideas for the magazine. Todd is full of ideas. Haven't you noticed him always writing in that notebook he wears around his neck? Why else would he try to hide it if it weren't good ideas?

CARTER: Oh, my god...I just realized. Those aren't ideas for new features...oh, my god.

TEMPLE: What now?

CARTER: Those are notes about us. He's the man who came to assess the staff. Johnson is the hatchet man!

TEMPLE: Are you sure?

CARTER: He writes down everything we do!...I admitted I can't write! He saw me sleeping! I talked to him about sex in the office. He knows everything about me.

TEMPLE: That little cipher is the hatchet man?

CARTER: And I just threatened to kill him. I'm done for!...I've got to win him back, the perfidious little swine...Which way did he go?

TEMPLE: Wait for me!

(CARTER *exits, limping and rushing.*)

(TEMPLE *exits, rushing out.*)

(TEMPLE's *office*)

(JOHNSON *enters, dejected from his session with Carter, but determined to try.*)

(JANE *looks up from her work, on her guard in the presence of a man.*)

JOHNSON: Hello.

(JANE *does not answer, eyes him warily.*)

(JOHNSON *enters and perches on the edge of* JANE's *desk.*)

JOHNSON: (*Continuing*) Those are lovely flowers....

JANE: Getawaydon'ttouch!

(JOHNSON *doesn't understand* JANE, *of course.*)

JOHNSON: I agree, probably...I like flowers, too.

(JOHNSON *makes a move as if to touch them.* JANE *snarls like a dog.* JOHNSON *recoils and gets off the desk.*)

JOHNSON: I notice your eyes are—yellow?...

JANE: Ididn'tmeantostartleyoubutthesefl owersareveryspecialtomeperhapswe shouldstartagain.

JOHNSON: (*Understanding nothing*) OoooKayyy...how's your mother?

(JANE *gives him the "up yours" sign.*)

JOHNSON: I...I... (*Sings*) Adieu, adieu, to yieu and yieu and yieu... (*He exits, singing but more dejected than ever.*)

(CARTER's *office*)

(SAM *enters.*)

SAM: Oh, Carter-Warter... (*She looks around, sees no one. She exits.*)

(TEMPLE's *office*)

(CARTER *enters, dashing in. His leg is better now.*)

CARTER: Is he here? Is he here?

(JANE *jumps to her feet.*)

JANE: Ohhhh. (*She holds out a rose and a handful of Post-its.*)

CARTER: Down, Jane, down.

(TEMPLE's *office*)

(TEMPLE *enters, rushing in.*)

TEMPLE: Have you seen Todd?

(JANE *indicates she gave him the "up yours" sign.*)

TEMPLE: (*Continuing*) He's the hatchet man!

JANE: Johnson?

TEMPLE: Don't panic, Jane! I have it!

(CARTER *notices the Post-its in* JANE's *hand.*)

CARTER: Oh, no! I left him a paper trail in my office telling him what he could do.

(CARTER *grabs the Post-its from* JANE, *finds one particular one.*)

TEMPLE: That was your death warrant.

CARTER: Not necessarily. I'll tell him you did it. (*He exits, rushing out.*)

TEMPLE: I need this job! I have allergies!

JANE: Johnson...hatchet man?

TEMPLE: (*Panicking*) Don't panic, Jane! I have it!

JANE: (*Panicked*) I'm not panicked!

TEMPLE: (*Panicked*) Why not?! Do you know something?

JANE: We're doomed!

TEMPLE: We can't leave Carter alone with him!

JANE: Run!

TEMPLE: Run!

JANE & TEMPLE: Run!

(*While trying to run,* JANE *and* TEMPLE *get in each other's way. They finally make it through the door and rush off.*)

(CARTER'*s office*)

(JOHNSON *enters. He pokes his head in cautiously, then enters.* JOHNSON *notices the first of the Post-its.*)

JOHNSON: (*Reading*) Quisling, this treachery... (*Next Post-it*) ...shall not pass... (*Next Post-it*) ...Pucker up and kiss my (*Next Post-it*) ...rosy red...

(CARTER *enters, rushing in.*)

CARTER: Johnson!

JOHNSON: I know, I'm going. (*Next Post-it*) ...rosy red...

(*As* JOHNSON *searches for the final Post-it,* CARTER *takes the Post-it that he took from* JANE *and slaps it on his chest. It won't stick so he picks up a pencil and tries to pin it to his chest with that. Only after he's stuck himself does he realize what he's done.*)

(JOHNSON *looks for the final Post-it [which is on the terminal, shielded by* CARTER's *body] sees* CARTER *gesturing mutely to his chest [and trying to stifle a scream]*).

JOHNSON: ...heart! (*Melting*) Carter.

CARTER: Johnson! Ben! My pal, my friend!

JOHNSON: Your friend?

CARTER: More than a friend, really. You must have sensed that I'm enormously fond of you. I don't always show it, I'm reticent by nature, but I think of you as more than a buddy. I think of you as a brother.

JOHNSON: (*Melting*) A b-b-brother?

CARTER: Like a twin, separated at birth.

JOHNSON: I've always wanted a brother.

CARTER: May I call you bro?

JOHNSON: I thought you were mad at me.

CARTER: That was merely an excess of my desire to do the very best I can for the magazine. Like champagne in a glass I just bubble up with enthusiasm for my work, can't help myself.

JOHNSON: You called me a Judas...

CARTER: In the best way.

JOHNSON: ...a swine and a traitor.

CARTER: In fun! We jest with one another in the office, we jest!

JOHNSON: I think fun is an important part of the office family.

CARTER: We can get together and throw a ball to each other...

(TEMPLE's *office*)

(OTIS *enters the empty office.*)

OTIS: Anyone for lunch? (*He exits.*)

(CARTER'*s office*)

(*Enter* TEMPLE, *rushing in.*)

TEMPLE: Todd! (*Points at* CARTER) Don't believe him!
Have I got ideas for you! Not like the things Carter...
(*She points at the computer to indicate* CARTER'*s work
and then sees the remaining post-it with the last word for
which* CARTER *substituted "heart". She is temporarily taken
aback.*)

(*Enter* JANE, *rushing in.*)

JOHNSON: Oh, there's more to the poem.

(CARTER *gasps.* JANE *sees the offending note and snatches
from the screen.* JOHNSON *reaches for the note.* JANE *puts it
in her mouth.*)

CARTER: (*Relieved and desperate*) Hungry, Jane? Must be
time for lunch!

(SAM *enters.*)

SAM: So, my bravos. Who's for the old feed-bag? Let's
saddle up.

(CARTER *puts his back to* JOHNSON *and mouths "thank
you" silently to* JANE. *He chastely kisses her on the head.
She grasps him around the waist and hangs on.*)

TEMPLE: (*Seductively*) Todd, let's you and I do lunch. I
have sooo many things I want to talk to you about.

CARTER: But he's promised me, haven't you, my
brother?

TEMPLE: No fair, you get him in your office all day. I
get so little time alone with you...Toddie.

CARTER: (*To* JOHNSON) Just us guys together, swapping
lies...

SAM: What the hell is this?

(JANE *whispers the truth in* SAM's *ear.*)

TEMPLE: I know the perfect place.

(JANE *takes Post-it from her mouth.*)

JANE: I'llgowithhim!

(JANE *releases* CARTER *and wraps herself around* JOHNSON's *waist.* CARTER *puts the post-it back in* JANE's *mouth.*)

(SAM *leaps into the spirit.*)

SAM: I hate to pull rank, but I think new man should have lunch with me.

JOHNSON: (*Overwhelmed*) Could...could we all eat together, like a family?

ALL: Oh, yes, please! Whatever you want!

JOHNSON: You want me to choose?

ALL: You know best! Tell us, tell us.

JOHNSON: Well...I don't know...I don't eat out very often. What is there?

CARTER: There's a great Mexican place.

JOHNSON: Mexican?

ALL: What a good idea, wonderful choice!

JOHNSON: Uh...Mexican?

ALL: Perfect! Love it!

JOHNSON: I may need a bib.

(TEMPLE *takes one of* JOHNSON's *arms,* CARTER *the other.* JANE *scurries around from side to side, trying to get hold of him, too, but* TEMPLE *and* CARTER *keep fending her off. They head towards the door.* JANE *manages to grasp him around the middle again.* SAM *comes from behind and massages his shoulders as they exit, rather like the entourage around a boxer entering the ring—except for* JANE *around his middle.*)

(*Exit all.*)

(*Pause*)

(*Enter* OTIS *to an empty room.*)

OTIS: No one for lunch? (*He looks around rather plaintively.*)

(*Black out*)

END OF ACT ONE

ACT TWO

Scene 3

(*Several days later*)

(JOHNSON *is seated at* CARTER's *desk, his feet up on the desk. He looks every inch a king and is obviously installed at the bigger desk now. He plays with some office toy.*)

(*Enter* JANE. *She carries coffee and a pastry which she offers to* JOHNSON *with the deference of a servant to royalty.*)

JOHNSON: Oh, how nice of you. Thank you, Jane... styrofoam?

(JANE *detects a tiny note of dissatisfaction.* JOHNSON *spells "styrofoam" in his unique sign language. He points to his eye for "sty", mimes rowing a boat for "ro", blows "foam" off of his coffee.*

JOHNSON: Styrofoam...I wonder why Temple always brings me a porcelain cup.

JANE: Mumble, mumble. (*She mouths "The Bitch!" to herself, then gives two thumbs up, indicates she can't wait to run errands for him and scoots out with the offending styrofoam cup.*)

JOHNSON: Only if you're going that way anyway.

(*Exit* JANE.)

(JOHNSON *takes out the red notebook and scribbles.*)

(*Enter* TEMPLE.)

(JOHNSON *quickly hides the notebook by collapsing over it so his head is almost on his desk.* TEMPLE *is dressed in a fashionable golf shirt and skirt and visor with pom-poms on her socks.*)

TEMPLE: Todddd...I'm not disturbing you, am I?

JOHNSON: Just thinking of a short nap.

TEMPLE: Of course. What a good idea. I was just going to ask your opinion—you know how I value your opinion—do you think this skirt is too revealing?

JOHNSON: Nah.

TEMPLE: (*Veiled annoyance*) Is it revealing enough?

JOHNSON: Up to you.

TEMPLE: Up to my what?

JOHNSON: Just going to rest my eyes for a few minutes.

TEMPLE: (*Crestfallen*) You're...indifferent, then? ...Oh...I'll go practice my golf swing while you rest. I have so many new and original ideas about the golf swing...If you'd like to come watch later...

(TEMPLE *takes a couple of clubless swings with an emphasis on her hip action. No response from* JOHNSON. *She leaves, very discouraged.*)

(JOHNSON *sits bolt upright and scribbles in his notebook.*)

(*Enter* OTIS.)

OTIS: Ah, Johnson. Beavering away, busy as a...an insect. Taking notes.

JOHNSON: No, no, I wasn't, honest.... (*He quickly stuffs the red notebook into a drawer.*)

OTIS: Letter home? Shopping list? Tic tac toe?

JOHNSON: No, no, just...some observations.

OTIS: Lay of the land, subtle chemistry, inner workings, that sort of thing.

JOHNSON: Well, sort of, yes. I do pay attention to detail. I think it's very important. It's how I bring order out of chaos.

OTIS: Well, for chaos you can't do better than here. How is the staff taking to you so far, gathering with torches at the castle walls, selecting stones of appropriate size?

JOHNSON: (*Complacently*) I've only been here a week and I've won all of them over—just charm, I guess—they treat me as one of the family now. More like a big brother, actually, seeking advice and so forth. Except for Sam. Sam is a little...

OTIS: Oh, my yes.

JOHNSON: Just a bit...

OTIS: I'll say.

JOHNSON: A little...

OTIS: Ouuuh.

JOHNSON: I haven't quite figured out what to do with her.

OTIS: Play dead, lie absolutely still, she'll lose interest. Worst thing to do is run...

JOHNSON: But once I get Sam figured out I've got them all sized up.

OTIS: Really? Quick as that.

(JOHNSON *makes a definitive key stroke at his computer.*)

JOHNSON: Well, my work here is finished.

OTIS: Done already?

JOHNSON: I like to get things over with quickly, why drag it out?

OTIS: Surgical cut, chop, like hacking through a chicken.

JOHNSON: Whatever you say. Now if you'll excuse me—

OTIS: Righty-oh, off you go. Hack, slash, salt the fields, take no prisoners.

(*Exit* JOHNSON.)

(TEMPLE'*s office*)

(*Enter* TEMPLE. *She carries a Medicus golf club. [The Medicus is a hinged training device that looks like a golf club but collapses on its hinge when swung improperly.] She tries to swing it, it keeps collapsing, to her bafflement.*)

(CARTER'*s office*)

(*Enter* CARTER.)

OTIS: Ah, Carter. Just having a chat with your friend Jackson. His work's all done.

CARTER: Oh, god. Did he say when?

OTIS: Just now.

CARTER: Did he say who?

OTIS: Taking notes.

CARTER: I've got to get hold of that damned notebook.

OTIS: Shouldn't be too hard. He locked it in the drawer.

(CARTER *frantically tries to open the desk drawer, first by pulling, then by prying with pencils, rulers, etc.*)

CARTER: (*As he struggles*) I knew I'd have to kill him eventually. I have toadied, praised, fawned...

OTIS: Should work.

CARTER: Groveled, sucked-up, kow-towed.

OTIS: Ought to be good enough.

CARTER: (*Still working frantically*) Otis, none of us can afford to lose our jobs! What other magazine would hire a writer who can't write? Temple has allergies.

Jane...Jane doesn't interview well.... Do corporations have to control everything? This company makes a profit, a corporation would demand that it make a fortune.

OTIS: Valid point.

CARTER: Small companies are a haven for the just so-so, the not-so-bad, the squeaker-by. That's most of us, isn't it? Here I'm surrounded by people in the same boat that I can annoy freely because they can't get away, the mutual misery of enforced labor...And damn it, we love it. Without it we'd have no lives at all...Oh, god, I need this job!

OTIS: Couldn't have put it better myself.

CARTER: I swear to you I'll kill him. You may want to avert your eyes.

(*In his desperation,* CARTER *is now standing on the desk and trying to pull the drawer open that way. He has his back to the door as* JOHNSON *enters.*)

CARTER: I'll skewer him like a shish kebab, grind his bones to bake my bread.

(*Exit* OTIS, *slipping out.*)

JOHNSON: Carter?

(CARTER *sees* JOHNSON.)

CARTER: Johnson! ...There you are, my honey. Otis and I were just talking about...Otis?

(*But* OTIS *is gone.*)

JOHNSON: What are you doing?

CARTER: Just looking for a notebook, my liege.

JOHNSON: My notebook?

CARTER: Do you have a notebook, too? I think I left mine in the drawer here when I bequeathed you my desk in a gesture of extreme friendship.

(JOHNSON *takes out key, unlocks drawer, removes his red notebook.*)

JOHNSON: I don't think there's anything else in there.

CARTER: Did you hear Sam?

JOHNSON: Where?

(JOHNSON *looks around in alarm.* CARTER *takes a wad of papers from his pocket and sticks it in the drawer while* JOHNSON'*s back is turned, then pretends to find it.*)

CARTER: Carefully concealed with the aid of packing tape and stuck to the... (*He withdraws a "notebook" of his own, the wad of loose papers held together by rubber bands.*) You see? We each have a notebook. Want to swap? I'll show you mine....

(JOHNSON *puts his red notebook on a chain around his neck.*)

JOHNSON: This isn't important.

CARTER: What interests you interests me, little brother, little Benjy Benjy Ben.

JOHNSON: (*Fondly*) It is amazing how close we've become, isn't it?

CARTER: Cain and Abel. And yet I felt this affinity from the first day you wandered in, looking as lost as a weasel in a shower stall. Ah, those carefree early days.

JOHNSON: At first I didn't understand the subtle interplay and dynamics, the sense of joy and fun and... well...romance...Can I ask you a favor? Unless it's against your principles...

CARTER: Bit of latitude there.

JOHNSON: I wouldn't ask you to do this but since we're such good friends...

CARTER: Siblings, D N A be damned.

JOHNSON: Go and steal the flowers from the reception area, would you? And take them to Temple with my compliments? And say something nice. One of those clever poems you do.

CARTER: You wish me to take the flowers to Temple. With your compliments.

JOHNSON: I know you used to like her a few days ago...

CARTER: Mere adoration, nothing more... But beautiful, sexy women are so often shallow, don't you find? Perhaps Jane would suit you better.

JOHNSON: Jane and I have a little trouble with communication. She keeps doing this... (*He demonstrates the "up yours" gesture.*)

CARTER: It's a friendly way of saying hello. Popular in the Mediterranean, I believe.

JOHNSON: No, Temple's been so—attentive— lately. It's kind of unmistakable. (*Chuckles*) Sort of embarrassing.

CARTER: I blush for you, mein Herr.

JOHNSON: But then everyone seems to have taken to me.

CARTER: None more than I, old buddy.

JOHNSON: I know. It's wonderful.... (*Pause*) What do you think?

CARTER: Milud?

JOHNSON: That little favor? Or don't you want to do it for me?

CARTER: I am gone, Sahib. (*He exits, cursing to himself.*)

(JOHNSON *takes out his red notebook and writes.*)

(TEMPLE's *office*)

(*Enter* OTIS.)

OTIS: Ah, Temple. Remarkable incident at the course today. Chap teed off without a ball...

TEMPLE: Otis...

OTIS: Not now, righty-oh, quite understand...

TEMPLE: (*Great interest*) No, no, keep going.

OTIS: Ahhh...lost the thread completely.

TEMPLE: You were talking about golf.

OTIS: Quite. Chap took a swing with a seven iron—no ball, mind—walked two huundred yards into the rough. "Sliced it," he said. Thought it peculiar myself, awfully long shot for a seven iron, but didn't want to put him off his game...

TEMPLE: Interesting...Otis, you like me don't you?

OTIS: Good Lord, absolutely lap dog for you. Romeo and the other fella.

TEMPLE: I'm so worried about this situation with Todd.

OTIS: Done his work already.

TEMPLE: Really?...

OTIS: Like chopping a chicken.

TEMPLE: Otis—You're the only one here who actually plays golf. I don't suppose you have any ideas about improving the magazine.

OTIS: Scads. Thought you'd never ask.

TEMPLE: Why didn't you tell anyone?

OTIS: Waiting for the highest bidder, ha-ha.

TEMPLE: Otis, I'm desperate, I'll do anything to keep this job. I can't work just anywhere. I have allergies, you know.

OTIS: Good Lord, one would never know. Had an allergy myself once. More of a rash, really. Chafed when I walked something fierce.

TEMPLE: Otis!

OTIS: My dear?

TEMPLE: Focus... Since we have so much in common, allergies and everything, would you consider sharing your ideas for the magazine with meee?

OTIS: Oh, well, pearls beyond price, don't you know. Nuggets of, um...

TEMPLE: (*Deep breath, stealing herself*) Otis, I'll do... anything. Do you follow me? ...I've always been fond of you, you know that.

OTIS: Ahh...missed a few of the indicators...

TEMPLE: Is there anything I can give you? Anything at all?

OTIS: Always open to negotiation. Been a long admirer of your...um...

TEMPLE: Yes, they are nice, aren't they? Why don't we meet and discuss this when no one can overhear us? Tonight? Here? At nine? Is that all right with you, just the two of us?

OTIS: Oh, I must say, eager as a...oh, builds dams...

TEMPLE: Silliness is a very attractive quality in a much older man.

OTIS: Oh, not that old. I've reached those attractive middle years. Still plenty of steam in the old whatnot...

TEMPLE: See you at nine, then... (*Caressing the name*) O-tisss.

OTIS: I'll just go loosen up, shall I? (*He exits, incredulous about his good fortune.*)

(TEMPLE *slaps her head in immediate regret for what she's gotten herself into.*)

(CARTER's *office*)

(*Enter* JANE. *She stalks up to* JOHNSON, *thrusts the porcelain coffee cup towards him.*)

JOHNSON: Ah, porcelain! Thank you!

(JOHNSON *gives* JANE thumbs up. She responds with "up yours!".

JOHNSON: I understand. (*He copies her "up yours" movement.*) Hi!

(JANE *looks at* JOHNSON *askance. Thinking she does not understand, he goes through the performance again, then gives her the "up yours!" sign as a gesture of happy farewell as she walks away from him in disgust. He winds up for a final "up yours".*)

(*Exit* JANE.)

(*Enter* SAM.)

(JOHNSON *mistakenly gives* SAM *the final "up yours".*)

JOHNSON: (*To* SAM) Oh, hello.

SAM: Happy to see me.

JOHNSON: Jane and I were just coming to an understanding. It takes a while.

SAM: Jane's a bit of a slow learner, but I like diligence in a man. Keep at it until you get the job done, that's what I like. (*She sits on his desk in a provocative pose.*)

JOHNSON: Ca...Ca...Carter isn't here.

SAM: Oh, I'm not here to see Carter. He's a silly boy, you know. Doesn't know a good thing when he has it spread-eagled in front of him...You, on the other hand, stick to a thing until you get it right, don't you?

JOHNSON: Yes, ma'am, that's my job. Assess the situation, analyze the factors involved, see what's required...

SAM: You are a real dark horse, aren't you?
   At first glance you look like a spavined exercise pony,

but, oh, the stories I hear about you. Otis says you've rounded the far turn and you're streaking into the home stretch, going to the whip with either hand.

JOHNSON: Ma...Ma...Ma'am?

SAM: Normally I like to bring my staff writers along slowly, take them under my wing, give them my tutelage, guidance...the odd bit of discipline, perhaps. I was going to treat you like that. (*She positions herself in a variety of poses that she thinks are sexy through the rest of the scene.*)

JOHNSON: Like a mother?

SAM: You miss the thrust, slightly. ...But suddenly, here you are, almost to the wire. I'm afraid you'll be at the finish line before we've even saddled up. You haven't give me a fair run, have you, Newman? I can ride with the winners, you know—I have the withers for it...

JOHNSON: R...Really?

SAM: You do like to ride, don't you?

JOHNSON: Sssspurs?

SAM: Certainly, if you like. You are a high-stepping strutter, aren't you? Don't you love horses, Newman? Don't you love all that quivering flesh, the strength and power in that superbly smooth muscle pulsing and throbbing under you, don't you love going bareback, don't you love when it rears up and demands to go and you're not sure you can handle it, you're not sure you can control it—but you can, you can! Oooowheee, doesn't it give you the shivers, just thinking about it?

JOHNSON: Well...yes...

SAM: Tell you what, come back to the office around nine tonight. We have so little time. We'll get to know each other—intimately—this way.

JOHNSON: I...I...I... (*Sings*) Harooo! The Continental...

SAM: We can try that, too... Nine o'clock. Don't disappoint me. (*She exits.*)

JOHNSON: (*Terrified*) Guh...Guh...Guh...Gupta?

(TEMPLE's *office*)

(CARTER *enters carrying the flowers from reception. He goes to one knee, offering the flowers.*)

CARTER: Oh, my angel, form divine
Accept these gifts as though they're mine...

TEMPLE: I'm allergic to those.

CARTER: They're from Johnson. Inconsiderate swine. (*He puts them on* JANE's *desk, disdainfully.*) That worm is under the impression that you like him.

TEMPLE: There's something fascinating about a man who can hand you your head on a plate, don't you think?

CARTER: The man is a slithy tove, he doesn't deserve you. Take me, instead... In fact, take me now.

TEMPLE: Oh, Carter, don't press me right now, I'm feeling very vulnerable...I've done a terrible thing.

CARTER: What?

TEMPLE: I can't tell you. You'll yell at me.

CARTER: I will swallow this before I yell at you, I promise... (*He indicates some object, an over-sized golf ball perhaps, that will fit in his mouth but is clearly not swallowable.*) All right, you don't want to talk about it with others in the office. Meet me here tonight at nine o'clock. I've got something to show you.

TEMPLE: But that's just it. I have an...engagement...with somebody else.

CARTER: Not that swine!

(TEMPLE *nods agreement.*)

CARTER: You!... (*Remembering his promise, he stuffs the golf ball in his mouth. At first he we hear the strangled sounds of his outrage, but those change to sounds of panic as he realizes the ball is stuck in his mouth.*)

TEMPLE: I had to do it. I think he can save my job.... Are you furious?

(CARTER's *noises turn to panic. He gestures to his mouth to show* TEMPLE *the ball is stuck. At no time does she realize he is in trouble. She assumes all of his gestures are in response to what she is saying.*)

TEMPLE: You mustn't take it personally.

CARTER: Gargle, snargle, bargle. (*He tries to pry the ball out using one finger.*)

TEMPLE: This doesn't mean I don't care for you. You're the reason I love coming to work.

(CARTER *puts his hands on his throat to indicate he's choking.* TEMPLE *thinks he means "me?". She nods and points a finger at him, meaning, "yes, you".*)

TEMPLE: Yes, you! You're so frantic, so blatantly insincerely sincere.

(CARTER *tries to pry the ball out with a pencil.*)

CARTER: Flanfurfarr!

TEMPLE: You won't hurt yourself because of this, will you?

(CARTER *nods head up and down, indicates he's hurting himself right now.*)

(CARTER *falls to his knees in front of* TEMPLE. *She thinks he's imploring her not to keep her date.*)

CARTER: Gargle, gargle!!

TEMPLE: I know, I know, me too. But I have to think of my job. Promise me you won't do anything rash.

(CARTER *shakes his head furiously side to side in a futile attempt to dislodge the ball.* TEMPLE *thinks he means he is indeed going to do something rash.*)

(*Finally* CARTER *manages to stagger out the door.*)

TEMPLE: (*Continuing*) No, you mustn't!

(CARTER *exits.*)

TEMPLE: Oh, what have I done?

(*Enter* JANE.)

JANE: Is Johnson half-witted, or what? He speaks in sign language. I hate a man who won't enunciate.

TEMPLE: Otis says the hatchet man is going to drop the ax right away. You'll be sure to go Jane, so if you have any last requests, put them in writing and I'll deal with it.

JANE: Me!? (*She notices the flowers on her desk.*) Who brought these?

TEMPLE: Carter, of course.

JANE: (*Hyperventilating*) Carter! Again?

TEMPLE: It happens so often I don't even tell you about it.

JANE: (*Melting*) ...Ooooh.

TEMPLE: He seemed suicidal when he left. I think he's given up hope.

JANE: (*Horrified*) No.

TEMPLE: All this time with no encouragement...

JANE: I must save him!

TEMPLE: Don't worry your head about it, Jane. I'll deal with it.

JANE: As if it's up to you. (*She scribbles a note, takes one of the flowers and starts towards the equipment door.*)

TEMPLE: Jane, what are you doing? Don't go in there!

JANE: Must hurry.

TEMPLE: You may never come out.

JANE: Have to try. (*She exits through equipment door.*)

(CARTER'*s office*)

(JOHNSON *puts the red notebook back in his shirt and leaves.*)

(*Exit* JOHNSON.)

(*Equipment door eases open a crack,* JANE *peeps in, sees the coast is clear and enters—with the attendant noise of falling equipment—and places the single flower and the note on* CARTER'*s desk.*)

(JANE *exits through equipment door.*)

(*Enter* CARTER, *with a pair of pliers. He uses the pliers to remove the ball from his mouth with a pop that drops him to his knees.*)

(CARTER *sees the flower on his desk, reads the note.*)

CARTER: (*Reading*) "Meet me here tonight at nine. Don't despair. I can resist you no longer."...She wants me! At last, Temple wants me! I've done it, I've worn her down! (*He puts the rose in his teeth, does a dance.*)

(*Enter* OTIS.)

OTIS: Oh, I say, Carter. You wouldn't have any quick ideas about the magazine, would you? Rather at a loss, myself.

CARTER: Tonight's the night, Otis.

OTIS: Indeed. Night of all nights.

CARTER: Big doings. Can't tell you what.

OTIS: Mum's the word.

CARTER: Won't mention the lady's name.

OTIS: Gentleman's code.

CARTER: This in no way diminishes my respect and affection.

OTIS: Finest of ladies.

CARTER: But I'll bring my knee pads.

OTIS: Let Mongo off the leash.

(CARTER *wordlessly mouths "Mongo?".*)

CARTER: Long time coming.

OTIS: Ooo—ooh. Nine's a bit of a stretch. Usually in bed by then...Take a nap now, then lots of coffee...

CARTER: Full frontal assault.

OTIS: Bound to come back to me, like riding a bicycle.

CARTER: Take no prisoners.

OTIS: Let Mongo feast tonight.

(CARTER, *again, mouths "Mongo?".*)

OTIS: The old boy's gone through a bit of a famine the last decade or so.

CARTER: Yes, well, whatever you're talking about, good luck to you, Otis.

OTIS: And to you, Carter.

(CARTER *and* OTIS *link arms and go out together.*)

CARTER: Into the fray.

OTIS: Tally ho!

CARTER: Tonight at last!

OTIS: Tonight!

(CARTER, OTIS *exit. Blackout*)

Scene 4

(*The stage is dark, it is night time.*)

(CARTER's *office*)

(*Enter* CARTER. *He turns on light. He carries something in a small duffel bag. He removes it and we see that it is an inflatable air mattress. He inflates the air mattress with a foot pump.*)

(*We hear a great commotion from the equipment room.* CARTER *freezes.*)

(*Enter* JANE *from equipment door. She staggers in, groping her way blindly because she has lost her glasses. Her clothes are disheveled, her hair is down.*)

JANE: Help! Is anyone there! I saw the light.... Hello? Hello? Where am I? How long have I been in there?

(CARTER *beholds* JANE *with horror, then slowly tip-toes towards the exit.*)

(JANE *wanders about, bumping into things.* CARTER *turns off the lights and exits. She responds to the loss of light.*)

JANE: What, what, w hat?

(TEMPLE's *office*)

(*Enter* OTIS. *He turns on the light. He is dressed in a blue blazer with a foulard at his throat.*)

(OTIS *carries flowers, a heart-shaped box of candy, a bottle of wine, two glasses, a silver candelabra with candles, all of which is a bit much for his coordination. Disaster threatens with each step.*)

OTIS: Anyone here? Came a bit early, thought it best to limber up. (*He manages to put the candelabra, flowers, candy, champagne and glasses on Temple's desk. He then proceeds to do some stretching. In a man of his age this should require a good deal of huffing and puffing and general failure.*)

(CARTER's *office*)

(*Enter* CARTER.)

(CARTER *turns the light on again.* JANE *can perceive light but not much else.*)

JANE: Is anyone there? Can you help me find my glasses, if you are there? Are you there?

(CARTER *tip toes towards his partially inflated air mattress. There ensues a ballet in which* JANE *nearly touches him with her outstretched hands but he eludes her with contortions, manages to get the air mattress and tip-toes out again. He turns off light.*)

(*Exit* CARTER.)

JANE: What, what, what? ...Must be on a timer. (*She finds a desk in the gloom and sits down, exhausted.*)

(TEMPLE's *office*)

(OTIS *completes his stretching. He is completely worn out.*)

OTIS: Pray for a second wind. Hopefully a following breeze, get my sails up...Too much coffee, tend to that at least. (*He exits, presumably to the bathroom.*)

(CARTER's *office*)

(JANE *rises from the desk and puts her foot in a wastebasket. Her foot is stuck. She gives up trying to free it and clomps around the room, one foot stuck in the wastebasket. Eventually she makes her way to the exit and goes clomping into the hall.*)

(*Exit* JANE.)

(TEMPLE's *office*)

(*Enter* TEMPLE.)

(TEMPLE *sees the wine, flowers, candy and candelabra on her desk.*)

TEMPLE: What have I done? I can't go through with this. (*She picks up the flowers and moves them to* JANE's *desk and begins to wheeze with an allergic reaction. Wheezing*) Haaa...haaaa...haaa... (*The wheezing is strong enough to freeze her in place for awhile. When she can get going again she hurries out of the office.*)

(CARTER's *office*)

(*Ener* SAM. *She turns on the lights. She is now sporting boots and a riding crop. The boots have spurs.*)

SAM: Anyone want to play horsie? ...A little hide-and-seek first, is it? (*She looks under the desks, etc, can't find anyone.*) That's all right, I like to make it hard. (*She exits, smacking herself with the crop.*)

(TEMPLE's *office*)

(*Enter* CARTER, *carrying his half-inflated air mattress. He notes the candelabra, wine, candy, etc on* TEMPLE's *desk.*)

CARTER: Oh, my sweet. You thought of everything. (*He puts the air mattress on the floor and starts pumping the foot pedal as fast as he can.*)

(CARTER's *office*)

(*Enter* JOHNSON, *rather glumly. He holds a small, limp bouquet of flowers. He looks morosely around the room. Doomed to his fate, he goes to his desk and sits.*)

(TEMPLE's *office*)

(CARTER *is pumping wildly when suddenly his leg injury acts up.*)

CARTER: (*Howling*) Owww, owww, owww... Not now!

(CARTER *falls onto the air mattress his bad leg in the air. We hear the clomp, clomp, clomp of* JANE *approaching in the hallway. He has no idea what the sound is until she enters.*)

(JANE *gropes forward, clomping, her hands in front of her.*)

JANE: Light, I see light. Is anyone here? Hello?

(*Using his hands and his one good leg,* CARTER *uses a swimming backstroke motion to slide himself and the air mattress towards the door. Again this requires a bit of a ballet to get past her. [N B: swimming on the air mattress is a bit ambitious. Carrying it while limping extravagantly will be easier to perform.]*)

(*Exit* CARTER, *sliding on his backside.* JANE *bumps into her desk, smells the flowers, finds them, touches them.*)

JANE: Oh, Carter. You've been here, my love.

(*Enter* TEMPLE. *She sees* JANE, *wastebasket and all, swooning over the flowers.*)

JANE: I will find you, I will find you, I will find you.

(TEMPLE *exits, tip-toeing away in horror.*)

(JANE *clomps around a bit and makes her way out.*)

(CARTER's *office*)

(JOHNSON *takes the red notebook from inside his shirt and writes in it.*)

(TEMPLE's *office*)

(*Enter* OTIS. *He sees the flowers on* JANE's *desk, moves them back to* TEMPLE's *desk, rearranges everything to his liking. He lights candles in the candelabra, then turns off the light. He begins a slow exercise/dance that might resemble tai chi as performed by a stork, for instance. He has his back to the door.*)

(*Enter* SAM. OTIS *has his back to her and is going through his gyrations in the gloom.* SAM *advances swiftly and gives him a swat on the butt with her riding crop.*)

SAM: (*Triumphantly*) Gotcha!

OTIS: Yow!

SAM: Otis!

OTIS: Sam?

SAM: What are you doing here?

OTIS: Ah. (*He immediately goes back into the awkward stork pose.*) Mik, mik, mik! (*He stands on left foot, right foot tucked behind left knee. His arms are akimbo. His head moves back and forth, first on one side, then the other.*)

(SAM *watches him in bewilderment.* OTIS *takes a step towards her, repeats his head motion.*)

SAM: You've finally snapped.

OTIS: It's the mating dance of the—oh, what do you call that thing? Mik. Mik. Mik.

SAM: Irishman?

OTIS: No, no. It mates for life.... Johnson would know, he loves animals.

SAM: That's a mating dance?

OTIS: Goose. The grey-lag goose. Mik, mik, mik. It gives them the stamina to mate for hours.

SAM: Now that's interesting. I didn't know you thought about such things, you old devil.

OTIS: More of a theoretical exercise, these days, still... Mik.

SAM: (*Touched*) You must find me very attractive.

OTIS: Hum? You? ...Oh, handsome woman. Still quite lovely—allowing for depreciation.

SAM: Keep dancing. I find it strangely alluring.

(OTIS *does a couple more moves as stork/goose.*)

OTIS: Mik. Mik.

(*In what* SAM *regards as a sexual signal of her own, she swats* OTIS *on the butt with her quirt again. This adds a little hop to his dance.*)

OTIS: Mik!

(*Swat, mik, swat, mik, swat. And thus they make their way out of* TEMPLE's *office.* OTIS *is not quite sure how he feels about the swats, but he doesn't object enough to tell her to stop.*)

(*Exit* SAM, OTIS.)

(CARTER's *office*)

(JOHNSON *is writing.*)

(*Enter* CARTER, *slithering in on the air mattress.*)

JOHNSON: Carter!

CARTER: Johnson, you villain! What are you doing here?

JOHNSON: N...n...nothing.

CARTER: How dare you coerce my beloved into having sex with you to keep her job.

JOHNSON: I...I...I...I didn't.

CARTER: Fiend! The proof is in your note book.

(JOHNSON *tries to hide his notebook.*)

CARTER: Give it to me! Give it to me!

(CARTER *tries to wrest the book from* JOHNSON, *which is hard on one good leg.*)

(*We hear clomp, clomp, clomp from the hallway.* CARTER *and* JOHNSON *stop wrestling to listen.*)

JOHNSON: It's Sam! She's come for me, I've made a terrible mistake! All I wanted was to be liked!

CARTER: Sam!

(*Together* CARTER *and* JOHNSON *hide behind a desk. We hear clomp, clomp, clomp outside in the hallway.*)

JOHNSON: She's got heavy weapons!

CARTER: Shhh!

(*The clomp, clomp, clomp comes close to the doorway.*)

JANE: (*Off; small voice*) Help...help...

(JANE *clearly has no expectation of help. The clomping stops, then resumes again, going away.*)

(*The men rise up from behind the desk—*CARTER *as best he can—and* CARTER *resumes his struggle for the book which becomes more lethal when he slips his hands down to* JOHNSON's *throat and starts to strangle him.*)

(*Suddenly we hear mik, swat, mik, swat.*)

(CARTER *and* JOHNSON *duck below the desk again.*)

(*Enter* OTIS, *running. He flattens himself against the wall next to the door. He is enjoying himself thoroughly.*)

(*Enter* SAM, *chasing. She overshoots, stops, looks around, does not see* OTIS *behind her. He, playfully, grabs her and gets her in a headlock.*)

OTIS: So you want to tussle, do you? Used to do my fair share of wrestling as a lad. I do a pretty wicked, oh, uh, what do you call it?

SAM: What the hell are you talking about?

(OTIS *has* SAM's *head locked in the crook of his elbow, holding her down around his waist.*)

OTIS: The wrestling hold. See here, it goes like this.

(OTIS *rubs his knuckles briskly against* SAM's *scalp. She squirms with pain.*)

(CARTER *and* JOHNSON *rise above the desk enough to watch this proceeding with shock.*)

OTIS: Now what's this called? Something French? No, no. Pitiful people, the Froggies.

SAM: Release me, you idiot!

OTIS: Dutch rub, that's it! ...This is a noogie, of course.

(OTIS *raps his knuckles on* SAM's *head, demonstrating a noogie. She yelps in pain with each rap.*)

(CARTER *decides to escape. Holding the air mattress under one arm, he hops on one foot, trying to time his hops so that* OTIS *and* SAM *don't notice him.*)

(*Exit* CARTER *with air mattress during* OTIS'*s wrestling.*)

(OTIS *gives* SAM *several more noogies as if she'd requested them, then releases her.*)

OTIS: There you are.

SAM: Well, now. That was interesting.... You must be really glad to see me.

OTIS: Delighted, as always.

(SAM *taps* OTIS'*s thigh.*)

SAM: What's that?

OTIS: Ah. That's my corkscrew.

SAM: I just bet it is. What's it good for?

OTIS: Opening wine bottles. Would you like to see it?

SAM: Yes, indeed.

(SAM *leans against a desk, wiggling her ass at* OTIS. *He manages to extract the corkscrew from his pocket and waves it triumphantly.*)

OTIS: Ta-da!

(JOHNSON, *horrified by the corkscrew and what might ensue, crawls from behind the desk and towards the equipment door.*)

(*Exit* JOHNSON *into equipment room.* SAM *hears the crash of equipment from the equipment room.*)

SAM: Is someone in there?

OTIS: I call him Mongo.

(We hear clomp, clomp, clomp, off.

JANE: (*Off, without hope*) Oh, help...oh, help.

SAM: We have to go somewhere else.

OTIS: Ah, just the place. (*He pulls her to the equipment door.*)

SAM: Not in there! Someone's in there!

OTIS: Well, he will be soon enough. I keep him with me wherever I go. Can't trust him on his own.

(OTIS *pulls the door and, miraculously, this time he does it right and it opens. He hustles* SAM *inside.*)

OTIS: Nothing to worry about, small problem with the light, a few blind alleys, culvert or two...

(*Exit* SAM, OTIS *into equipment room with noise off of crashing equipment.*)

(*Enter* JANE, *clomping in.*)

(JANE *gropes her away around. Inadvertently she hits the light switch and turns off light.*)

JANE: What, what, what?

(TEMPLE'*s office*)

(*Enter* TEMPLE. *She is no longer wheezing. She takes a deep breath, holds it, then transfers the flowers from her desk to* JANE'*s desk again. Back at her desk she tries to open the wine bottle with pencils, paper clips, etc. She if finally reduced to gnawing at the cork.*)

(*Enter* CARTER, *hopping, holding the air mattress, swinging his bad leg like a pendulum.*)

TEMPLE: Carter?

CARTER: There you are, my angel, at last.

TEMPLE: Why are you jumping around like that?

CARTER: Hopping with joy to see you.

TEMPLE: Are you infirm?

CARTER: Hardly. (*He drops the air mattress to the floor.*)

TEMPLE: Have you seen Otis?

CARTER: We may have seen the last of Otis. I think he's about to play Dobbin to Katherine the Great.

TEMPLE: What on earth are you talking about?

CARTER: Never mind...Otis won't trouble us.

TEMPLE: Oh, Carter, thank you. You came to rescue me, didn't you?

CARTER: Uh...we can call it rescue. (*He sweeps the flowers from* JANE's *desk and offers them to her, putting them in her face.*) They don't do you justice, and yet...

TEMPLE: (*Wheezing*) Haaa...haaaa...haaa...

CARTER: You're overcome by the gesture. I understand.

(TEMPLE *backs away from the flowers, wheezing, holding her hands in front of her to fend* CARTER *off. He pursues her with the flowers. She makes the sign of the cross with her fingers as if confronted by a vampire.*)

TEMPLE: Haaa...haaaa...haaa... (*She exits, wheezing.*)

CARTER: Temple...don't make me chase you... (*He takes a few tentative hops, then stops.*) I give up. I quit, I'm through. That's the last time you torment me.

(*Enter* OTIS *through equipment door in* TEMPLE's *office.* OTIS *manages to get only his head through the door.*)

CARTER: Not now, Otis.

OTIS: Good God, man! Have pity!

(OTIS *is yanked back into the equipment room.*)

(CARTER *flops down on the mattress on his back, holding the flowers like lilies on a corpse.*)

(CARTER's *office*)

(*Enter* JOHNSON *from equipment door. He turns on light.*)

JANE: (*Startled*)	JOHNSON: (*Startled by* JANE)
What,	What,
(*Continuing*)	(*Continuing*)

what,	what,
(*Continuing*)	(*Continuing*)
what?	what?

JANE: You're here at last! I've been looking everywhere for you.

  I've waited for you so long, I've loved you from afar, there, I've said it, I don't care because I know you've felt that way too but were too shy to say so, I understand shyness, it's been the curse of my life, but we've put that behind us at last, and here we are and come to me my darling and take me in your brawny arms, let me rip fistfuls of hair from your back as you ravish me with your unbridled lust, thrusting, thrusting, come to me, come to me...WHERE THE HELL ARE YOU!

JOHNSON: Uh...I...I... Yi...

JANE: Shut up and kiss me, you fool!

(JANE *puts her head back, opens her arms, puckers in a classic pose.* JOHNSON *thinks a moment, shrugs, then kisses her. She wraps herself around him, arms, legs, wastebasket and all in a huge kiss that will last until we return.*)

(TEMPLE's *office*)

(*Enter* TEMPLE, *no longer wheezing.*)

TEMPLE: Okay, continue.

CARTER: With what?

TEMPLE: Say something beautiful and desperate. I need to hear that right now.

CARTER: Nah. I'm through. I'm tired of making a fool of myself over you. I'm tired of feeling as if I'm going to burst every time I look at you. Let the other fools do it. You've worn me out.

TEMPLE: ...You really feel like you're going to burst? That's so sweet.

CARTER: No, it's not. It's painful. It feels like something is sucking the breath out of your lungs. It makes you dizzy, it makes you panic, it makes you act like an idiot.

TEMPLE: But Carter...I didn't think you cared, I thought you were an idiot.

CARTER: I've been stupid, chasing after a woman who thinks of me as a moron. And tonight you're just toying with me again. Well, I said I had something to show you... (*He digs in his pocket.*) And here it is. (*He pulls out his wad of notes.*)

TEMPLE: What is it?

CARTER: What you wanted, isn't it? Ideas for the magazine. I've been saving them for years.

TEMPLE: Why?

CARTER: To give to you. I thought there might come a time when we could share them...but take them, it doesn't matter anyway. It's not the content of the magazine that matters. It's the graphics, the layout, the cover. Do you have enough articles with numbers in the title? Thirty ways, sixteen secrets, forty-two reasons.

TEMPLE: (*Of notes, surprised*) Carter, these ideas are good! I've misjudged you. Why, with ideas like these, a woman could, we could...

CARTER: Take them. I tried to throttle Johnson because of you, he has to fire me now anyway.

TEMPLE: Oh, how can I ever thank you?

CARTER: Really... Well...as a parting gesture...

(TEMPLE *kisses* CARTER. *He tries to get her onto the mattress.*

TEMPLE: Not here. There are people in the office.

CARTER: I have just the place. (*He leads her to the equipment door, then hops back and grabs the mattress.*)

(*Exit* TEMPLE, CARTER *through equipment door.*)

(CARTER's *office*)

(*The kiss between* JOHNSON *and* JANE *ends.*)

JANE: I knew you'd be a wonderful kisser, you have such trembling lips!

(JOHNSON *removes the wastebasket from her foot while kneeling before her.*)

JANE: Oh, my hero... Kiss me there, right there.

(JOHNSON *kisses* JANE's *calf.*)

JANE: And there, and there...

(JANE *works* JOHNSON *up her leg a bit. He obliges.*)

JANE: You know just what to do for me. Take me now, you brute. Take me, take me!

(JOHNSON *looks around for a place to take her, then leads her to the equipment door.*)

(JOHNSON, JANE *exit through equipment door.*)

JANE: (*Continuing; off*) What, what, what?

(*Everyone is in there now. Black out*)

Scene 5

(*Lights up almost immediately. Sufficient time has passed.*)

(*Both offices are empty. From the equipment closet we hear various yips and sighs and animal noises.* JANE's *voice soars in a "Haarooo!" as all the noises come to a climax.*)

(TEMPLE's *office*)

(*Enter* OTIS, SAM, *holding hands. She carries the air mattress.*)

SAM: Oh, Otis, this was so good for me. Younger men are so obsessed with their performance.

OTIS: Callow youth.

SAM: But not you, Otis. You don't care how you perform.

OTIS: Not a bit...eh?

SAM: Did you like what I did with your toes?

OTIS: My toes? Concentrating more on the ripping of hair off my back. Oddly stimulating.

SAM: Hair? Well, it doesn't matter.... Oh, Otis, I've been so lonely.

OTIS: Have you, my dear? So have I.

SAM: It's so hard to meet any suitable men at my age. Men are all so young, these days.

OTIS: Yes, well...

SAM: Except for you, Otis.

OTIS: Very kind.

SAM: But that doesn't matter now. Tell me all about yourself.

OTIS: Ah, well, where to start? Born in the usual way, dark of night, mother cursing father, prophesies, divinations...

(*Exit* SAM, OTIS, *holding hands.*)

(CARTER's *office*)

(*Enter* TEMPLE, CARTER *from equipment door. She carries the riding crop.* CARTER *has his arm around her.*)

CARTER: Wow!

TEMPLE: I'm glad.

CARTER: And you?

TEMPLE: You were probably nervous...Just one question. When you had your head on my shoulder and were whimpering like a sissy...

CARTER: Wouldn't word it quite like that...

TEMPLE: ...how did you manage to do that thing with my toes at the same time?

CARTER: Toes?

TEMPLE: That was wonderful.

CARTER: Ah, well. We aim to please.

(*Enter* JOHNSON, JANE *from the equipment door.*)

(*Somehow* JOHNSON *has managed to get* JANE's *chain and glasses around his neck and she has his red notebook and chain around her neck, hanging down her back. She is draped all over him.*)

CARTER: Johnson?

(JANE *recognizes* CARTER's *voice, but doesn't understand why it's not coming from the body she clings to.*)

JANE: Carter?

TEMPLE: Jane?

JOHNSON: Temple?

JANE: Who? (*She squints at* JOHNSON, *still can't make him out. She tries to feel his face to figure it out, and in the process comes across her glasses which she removes from his neck and puts on during the following.*)

(*Enter* OTIS, SAM, *holding hands.*)

TEMPLE: Otis?

CARTER: Sam?

SAM: Carter?

OTIS: Temple?

(JANE *manages to get her glasses on, realizes she's been with* JOHNSON *all this time.*)

JANE: Johnson?

JOHNSON: Jane. You and me?

JANE: And mother?

JOHNSON: I've always wanted a mother!

CARTER: So what now, hatchet man? Are you going to fire us all?

JOHNSON: Hatchet man? I'm not a hatchet man.

TEMPLE: Then how do you explain this? (*She grabs the red notebook hanging down* JANE's *back, nearly garroting* JANE *in the process. She holds it up triumphantly.*)

JOHNSON: Don't look, don't look!

(CARTER *grabs the red notebook, garroting* JANE *again. He opens and reads it.*)

CARTER: Ha-ha!... (*Puzzled*) What is this?

(TEMPLE *grabs red notebook,* JANE *garroted.*)

TEMPLE: It looks like...notes for a novel?

SAM: (*Approvingly*) You're writing about us?

OTIS: (*Pleased*) In a novel?

TEMPLE: Well...that's all right.

JOHNSON: (*Ashamed*) It's not for a novel...it's for a play.

SAM: (*Appalled*) A play.

OTIS: Good Lor, Johnson. The theater?

TEMPLE: Who goes to plays?

OTIS: All that—talk. How do they remember it?

JANE: (*To* JOHNSON) How could you?

CARTER: Does this mean you're not the hatchet man? ...Then who is?

OTIS: Ah...well...not to put too fine a point on it, me, I. When the mater passed, I inherited the majority share of the magazine.

Thought it wise to take a closer look at the way things work. So I slipped into your midst, cunning as a...oh, dog-like creature...

(*The others are stunned into momentary silence.*)

CARTER: ...what have you concluded?

OTIS: Well, at first I thought I might have to sack the lot of you, but something—a thing—has come over the office lately. Carter is writing better...

(CARTER *embraces* JOHNSON.)

CARTER: Thank you, bro.

TEMPLE: I have ideas! (*She waves the notes, then hugs* CARTER.)

OTIS: ...Jane has become more voluble...

JANE: (*very rapidly but intelligibly*) Idon'tknowwhype oplethoughtIwasshy I'mnotsoshyamIJohnson... (*She embraces* JOHNSON.)

OTIS: ...And Sam is friendlier—quite affectionate, actually, in a very vigorous way—

(SAM *gooses* OTIS.)

SAM: Oh, Otis.

OTIS: So I've decided to keep the magazine the way it is. And of course one person gets credit for all of this.... Give credit where it's due...

(*Everyone clusters around* JOHNSON *saying, yes, yes, yes.*)

OTIS: But, no need for thanks. Happy to help, just doing my job. Now what say we all go out for a drink?

(*General chorus of yes, yes, hooray, good idea.*)

OTIS: I think the Mexican place is still open.

(*They all go trooping happily out together without including* JOHNSON *in the general enthusiasm. He stays behind, excluded again.*)

(JOHNSON *is alone again and crestfallen.*)

(*Pause*)

(*Enter all.*)

JANE: Johnnie.

TEMPLE: Todd.

CARTER: Come on, bro.

SAM: Bottoms up.

OTIS: Kenneth, lad.

(JOHNSON, *now our beamish boy, goes to the outstretched arms of the others.*)

JOHNSON: I...I...I...

ALL: (*Singing*)
Harooo, the Continental, it's very daring
The Continental, it's strictly *entre nous*
The Continental, it's very subtle
Because it does what you want it to do...
(*If needed*)
It has a passion, the Continental
An invitation to moonlight and romance.
It's quite the fashion, the Continental
Because you tell of your love while you dance...
Ooooh, You kiss while you're dancing, it's continental
And you will do the Continental all the time.

(*Exeunt omnes, singing.*)

(*Curtain*)

END OF PLAY

.

www.ingramcontent.com/pod-product-compliance
Lightning Source LLC
Chambersburg PA
CBHW070024110426
42741CB00034B/2444